Great Is Thy Faithfulness

When Our Faith Is Shaken

James E. McReynolds, Th.D., D.Div., Litt.D., Psy.D., Ph.D.

Minister of Joy to the World

Parson's Porch Books

Great Is Thy Faithfulness: When Our Faith Is Shaken
ISBN: Softcover 978-1-960326-33-1
Copyright © 2023 by James E. McReynolds

Parson's Porch Books is an imprint of Parson's Porch *&* Company (PP*&*C) in Cleveland, Tennessee. PP*&*C is a self-funded charity which earns money by publishing books of noted authors, representing all genres. Its face and voice is **David Russell Tullock** who you can contact at: dtullock@parsonsporch.com.

Parson's Porch *&* Company *turns books into bread & milk* by sharing its profits with the poor.

www.parsonsporch.com

Great Is Thy Faithfulness

DEDICATION

To the people who have sought God's salvation when the Holy Spirit has
touched them with love
and grace through faith even when their faith has been shaken.

Contents

FOREWORD

"Faith means to be overwhelmed by the reality of God."

James McReynolds says that in this marvelous book. What a statement it is, and how strongly it resonates in our hearts and minds.

Jim was a student of mine many years ago at Vanderbilt University. He is now in his 80s. That makes his statement all the more shining and remarkable. He knows whereof he speaks.

He has lived the life of faith and can talk about it with the surety and confidence few authors are able to exhibit today.

Like Jim's other books, this one resounds with memorable truths that are the product of his own experience. I'm an old man too— a few years older than Jim—and I know how important it is, especially in books of a spiritual or religious nature, for the author to speak not out of imagination or mere conjecture but out of his own deep and valid experience.

I find the truths in this book extremely important for the way they bolster and enlarge upon the truths in my own experience.

That is what religion and faith are really about—not mere pipe dreams of the soul, but realities of life drafted after years of trial and error, of wrestling with the hard facts of human existence as they manifest themselves in day-to-day living.

Faith is not something we have in isolation from the other aspects of our living. When we have it, it is the central fact of our being, the heart and soul of our lives. It radiates into everything we do and are.

Jim reminds us in this book of something very important, that the great old truths of biblical understanding—things like faith, love, hope, and joy—have in many cases become so familiar to us, and we speak of them so casually and repetitively, that they often lose something of their shivering reality for us.

They become mere slogans mere shibboleths, and we utter them with such ease and familiarity that they eventually possess a mere fraction of their reality.

What Jim attempts to do for us readers are to call us back to the full power of the words and what they mean, to renew our sense of their true reality, which is so much bigger and more dynamic than we remember.

He does this with incredible skill and cleverness, so that at some point in reading his books we begin truly to believe again, and to sense and appreciate the depth and passion of the pillars of Christian faith and understanding.

He accomplishes this remarkable feat in many ways, often with quotations and stories that have the power to revitalize the fuller meaning of our beliefs.

I am always amazed at the breadth and depth of both his vast reading and his memory, and the variety of the very apt quotations he cites. His stories are amazing too.

He is obviously a conservationist, who has preserved all kinds of information that are capable of enhancing the meaning of what we already know, so that we feel stimulated and enriched by reading only a few pages of his text.

This is an extremely rare gift, and I commend Jim's many books to any new reader who has yet to discover it. Thank you, Jim, for sharing your insights with us. We cannot read even a few pages of what you have written without becoming richer, deeper, more thoughtful Christians—in short, without having more faith.

Dr. John R. Killinger Warrenton, Virginia

INTRODUCTION

Richard Niebuhr said of faith: "Faith is the attitude of the self in its existence toward all existences that surround it, as being relied upon or to be suspected. It is the attitude that appears in all the wariness and confidence of life as it moves about among the living. It is fundamentally trust or distrust in the being itself." (H. Richard Niebuhr, *The Responsible Self,* p. *118)*

People have suffered and enjoyed, lost and won, doubted and believed, regressed and progressed on their faith journey. Ask anyone who has faith, has known doubt. Christian writers possess quiet confidence. This writer sees faith as the complete trust in the God of the gospels. Each human experience is different, but the points of trust as the same.

Failure Is an Invitation to Faith

We shun failure because we fear that revealing our weaknesses and imperfections will cause us to be unacceptable, unlovable, and of no use, unmarketable. Failure exposes our vulnerability. Failure is part of humanity. Being human challenges us to recognize life as a gift. Difficulties and failures have essential things to offer us. Children learn to walk by trying, failing, and trying again.

Mistakes, errors, failures are ways to learn to live life more fully. God proceeds to stay with us when we are raw and vulnerable, moving in our being with deep care and gentleness. Failure can lead us to the light.

We are more attentive when life is hard. Stretching our spirits, now worn and fragile from the pain of failure, we receive love and comfort. We must encounter failure. We need to embrace it. We always have and we always will. The earth where we exist, has been in existence for a long time. Humans have been around one-third as long as the universe. Earth's story began about five billion years ago. More than 600 million years was taken for the earth's crust to take shape. It too 300 million years more for the first signs of microbial life to begin. After numerous mass extinction events and 465million years later, mammals finally arrived.

Modern humans did not exist for another 70 million years. We humans first appeared about 300,000 years ago. During a public planetary talk, we learned that humans have only been on planet earth for 0.0067 per cent of its existence.

Humans were at first nomads. We learned to harness fire. Civilizations took shape. Unbelievably, humans have been on a meteoric trajectory, going from hunters to space wanderers in less than 6,000 years.

Trust and mistrust are ways we relate to our parents and others beginning early in life and running deeply all the years of our lives. I enjoyed Jennifer Lawrence's movie, *Joy*. Lawrence plays a lovely young woman who believes in our self. She envisions and creates a simple mop. Nobody thinks it will ever be a success. She is strong and despite her many disappointments and pain, she gains faith and success. Failure was her friend. She acknowledge he failure without becoming trapped by it.

Reflection enables us to remain responsible, spiritual, emotional, and practical. Failure offers us an opportunity to look and ask and delve into who we are. How do we desire to live life. We don't feel valued by our culture, church or community, or even ourselves. God's love and grace helps us love ourselves. Loving ourselves includes struggling with jealousy and envy toward others whose lives appear easier and more successful than ours. We reflect alone and with others. Sharing experiences of failure with people who know and love us provides encouragement in our times of darkness.

To pray is to reflect the reality and truths about us, others, the world, and God. This does not mean possessing, having, or consuming. In prayer we encounter God intimately. God reminds us that we are precious. Isaiah 43:4-5.

Prayer provides solace in our pain. It quiet our spirits so we move past the surface answers and self-deception to hear the deepest desires of our souls. The power we have is the power of the spirit within us. Failure can bring relief.

If we know that we can never be perfect, we finally get off our backs. I am accepting of my gifts and my work and willing to try different and new things. We confuse incompleteness with failure. Our world is filled with instant gratification and the quick fix. We quickly use the label "failure."

Failure reminds us to look back with gratitude for God's faithfulness in the past. We look forward in anticipation to the eternal joy that can become ours. Failure invites us to gather bot the past and future into the present moment that we live fully and faithfully now.

The challenge of failure is for us to remain faithful despite our fears, in the middle of the grief, loss, and pain, embarrassment, insecurity, and disappointment.

We become even further graced as we grow with compassion, wisdom, and love. If you think you have failed completely with no hope, please read this book, and give a copy to others.

Remember Jesus failed. We live on this side of the resurrection, so we miss the anguish and pain of the failure that proceeded it. The world would think that the life and ministry of Jesus were failures. He did not change the hearts of all those who heard him. He was not the type of messiah that brought the reign of God on earth. Jesus even failed to gain the complete loyalty of his disciples. They denied any association with him.

Jesus died as a common criminal. He died lonely, in much pain, ridiculed, and taunted. The challenge of faith and faithfulness is to hold that fruit of the Spirit within us, whatever life brings. That is the reality of faith.

Faithfulness and Responsibility

Faith is always somewhat off balance as it ventures forward into the new. Writers have to buy and try to sell their own self-published books. Parson's Porch Books has published many beautiful books. I have given many away to others. Artists offer their painting in poor artist shows on the street. They risk their capital. Risking is to put faith to the test. Life finds joy and excitement as we run risks. God is interested in how we handle what belongs to another. That is a test of our faithfulness. Never waste the resources of others because these are not ours. If we are not faithful to what belongs to others, we hinder ourselves from receiving from God what will be our own. Luke 16:12.

How we spend money that belongs to others is a characteristic of faithfulness. Never squander it just because it is not your own. Even if she or he acquires such money legibly, all involved are responsible.

Renting another's home or managing other people's property teaches a person how to manage property. An unmarried young woman is faithful to help her mother, sisters or brothers in caring for children before she marries becomes a blessing in disguise.

Whatever we become we are now becoming. If we are unfaithful with what belongs to others. If we are lazy in another person's business, we won't be diligent when we are trying to establish our own. I Corinthians 4:2. Anybody wasting what belongs to another will later waste what belongs to him or her.

God demands our faithfulness with what belongs to others. Work as if you are working for God and not another human being. God will reward us for the good we do. Ephesians 6:6-8, Colossians 3:25:19.

An unfaithful person is unreliable. Nobody wants to continue a relationship with such a person. Proverbs 25:19.

We all find hope in the story of Abraham and his never settling down. He went into unknown territory. My dad built a new home after coming back from the Pacific Theater during World War II. He had a job paying $37.50 per week and a G.I. loan.

He somehow was able to construct a two-story brick home at 1300 Edgemont Avenue in Bristol, Tennessee where Viking Hall, an arena for basketball, now stands. My father designed the home, did all the plumbing, hammered every nail, got brick discarded when the TVA dam was built. The home was later moved near the South Holston Lake near Bristol.

My father believed that each person must build their own home in his own way, molding it as he goes along. Faith is not good if it is imposed or transmitted.

The vision of a church filled with joy will focus the eyes of faith on Jesus the Christ, whose glory God is revealing. Along life's journey, we are sustained by faith. Most of us are eager to know and experience more. Congregations are given the opportunity for people to say to one another where they are in their seeking faith. The church of joy gathers and scatters their faith. Enriching life for one multiplies to the whole church or spiritual meeting and sharing.

Childhood church experiences are stories filled with a differing mix. Sunday School teachers are given much more credit than pastors. Children remember the kindness, love, and faithfulness.

My own experience with church was both positive and negative. Our memories include church splits over pastors, conflicts over correct doctrine, a nagging sense of guilt, boring sermons and lessons. The church was the extended family.

Most people saw church as their social as well as spiritual aspects of living. Most people who lived near my church in South Bristol were poor. Birthday parties, social meals, family reunions, youth dates, even sports teams like softball or youth basketball, bowling, playing church, or anything else that brought some surprising joys and pleasures in the midst of the sadness that being economically deprived brought a host of ordinary people with struggles and poor health.

Faith was often shaken. Physicians were not available. Teeth stayed crooked. Babies had no milk. Some children had no adequate schools. Only those with money were on organized Little League teams.

My friend John Killinger once in a sermon talked about the plight of a poor child at Christmas, "I ate my orange and blew up my balloon, and it was over."

The reason I wrote this book on faith and faithfulness is the tremendous need for humankind to cope with and understand it.

As we begin, let me share some words printed for visitors and members of Eastridge Presbyterian Church in Lincoln, Nebraska:

"God's love creates a beautiful world, but our distortion and denial of his love lead to life's degradation.

"God does not give up on us or any creature, and so God works to redirect our waywardness, so that we can participate with God in the healing of all life.

"The goal of God's love is for it to be fully active in the life of each and every creature. When that happens, life becomes heavenly." (Norman Wirzba, *Way of Love: Recovering the Heart of Christianity* p.42)

These words are used as the vision for Eastridge Presbyterian Church in Lincoln, Nebraska. These words can give you assurance about faith and faithfulness.

C.S. Lewis' faith experience including being raised in church. Soon as a young adult, he stopped believing the things his church taught.

As we wait and hope in God, God is already changing us. We have no idea what great things God is doing below the surface, but we believe that God is working for our good. We may not see it clearly now, but some day face to face, it will be revealed. So let us wait in hope. During worship on a Sunday, I sang with the congregation, "Faithful you are. Faithfully forever you'll be. All your promises are yes and amen." Psalm 4:6-7, Psalm 119:162, Jeremiah 15:16.

Celebration and Faith

Faith means celebration. It is a harbinger of heaven when we sing the songs of faith.

Think back to the last birthday party you may have celebrated. "Happy Birthday" is a glad song whether we are one or one hundred. Singing is quite natural with friends during a concert, at a funeral. Singing with a congregation setting has been widely accepted among various denominations.

God commands us to sing. There are many passages of scripture that refer to singing. Faithfulness involves singing. In the history of the church, Christians record singing. They expressed their beliefs in songs.

Songs have been the source of our theology. Church hymns throughout the ages are full of theological texts. Singing uses both left and right sides of the brain.

Singing connects us emotionally. Songs of celebration connects us emotionally. Singing leads us to dance. Lamenting hymns bring tears to our eyes. Psalm 96.

In I Samuel 7:12, we read that Samuel set down a stone and gave it a name," Ebenezer." Ebenezer meant "stone of help." The stone was a remembrance of the faithfulness of God.

I enjoy collecting rocks: pretty rocks, unusual, shaped rocks, heart shaped rocks, rocks collected during my world travels. I have hundreds of them in my collection.

I write on them where I found it and the date. They celebrate God's work in my life. They become a record of my personal relationship with God. I find joy in remembering the sanctification God has gracefully placed in my life.

On some stones I have written the name of a church and the date I preached in that community. I have stones with hospital names on them, where I or my family sought the help for healing bodies.

Stones celebrate my 70 years in ministry and where my Lord has taken me in my career. The joy of the Lord has been my strength, and my rock collection is like my Ebenezers, celebrating the faithfulness of God and how far God has taken me.

Remembering God's help in the past is important. Each time we as God's people remember how God helped us in the past, there is a sense in which we "raise our Ebenezer, our Stone of Help."

With joy I recall singing, "Here I raise my Ebenezer; Hither by thy help I've come; And I hope, by thy good pleasure, safely to arrive a home."

God who has delivered us "thus far" is the same God who will deliver us "thus forward." Ebenezers are the touchstones of our faith.

During the 11 years that I served as pastor for the First Christian Church in Weeping Water, Nebraska, one grateful young man constructed a huge stone with a red chalice on it for us to see it as a historical marker of how God blessed us.

It has become a boundary with spiritual meaning. Samuel sought to keep the memory of God's deliverance current in the minds of the ones who would be living in the future.

Large rocks and stones were used to mark significant eras in the ancient world. The stones were sometimes named and believed to stand for divine protection.

The name given and the physical memorial undoubtedly is a confession of faith in God. Simple stones collected remind me of the faithfulness of God in my life. Stroking them is touching my own Ebenezers. I then whisper quietly, "Thus far God has helped me."

Creating occasions for remembering is important in the lives of people and places. Stone memorials such as the one with a red chalice on it in Weeping Water gives us stability in the present and hope for the future as we are reminded how God was with us in the past.

Each person and every church and every community has reminders of their timelines of faith. Every time the people of Israel looked back at that stone, it reminded them that God had been faithful before and would be faithful again. We must remember God's grace in our lives. Revival times have come and gone. Beloved pastors are not there.

There is no evidence that the Israelites continued to build after the era of the Ebenezer. The euphoria of being a church of joy with our stone memorials cannot last. There are no stories about called ministers drawing from the landmarks.

In our humanity, we tend to forget how good God has been to us. God has taken us by the hand and has led us through dark times and many storms, paths of pain and doubt.

Every child of God has her and his Ebenezer for remembering God's faithfulness. Thee stones anchor them into the promises of God in the middle of painful, difficult, frightening, and challenging circumstances.

God turns disasters into blessings. God leans in and listens to their prayers. God has protected, rescued, and provided through each and all generations.

God holds our tomorrows just as our yesterdays. God knows what we will face in the future. Because when pain in life becomes severe, we can look at our memorial stone set in place in a time of strength.

Overwhelming Faith

"Faith is man's response to God's initiative," wrote John White. To realize that faith is your response to something God does or says, will take pressure off you and enable you to adopt a more constructive attitude.

"Do not look inside yourself and ask, 'How much faith do I have?' When Jesus praised the faith of different women and men in the gospels, he was not praising a mystical inner state. He was responding to a concrete action of the Roman centurion who sent his servants to Christ asking only that Christ speak the word of power. Faith was the person's response, usually in overt action, to God's call. (John White, *The Fight*, pp. 23-24)

Making a public decision to accept Christ is a relationship issue. We are sensitive to God's heart when we develop a friendship with our Creator. If our congregation is a Church of Joy, we will hear the voice of God within the context of our spiritual relationships. Walking with Jesus enables us to understand God's intentions for us and the world.

Salvation Takes Time

During revivals or spiritual gatherings, we want to make a right and lasting decision. Decisions are issues of trust. Psalm 103:13-14.

When I made my own decision to accept Christ, it was during a Vacation Bible School at the age of eight in Woodlawn Baptist Church in Bristol, Tennessee. What lay ahead of me and the other children who made their decisions for Christ was unknown.

None of us will ever know the future. James 4:13-17. We step out in faith. The will of God concerns the present more than the future. In fact each day we are "being saved." Eternal salvation takes time. II Peter 1:5-9.

We must permit our children to make their own choices. The will learn the consequences of poor choices. Scripture consistently reveals that we are God's children.

God calls us all to mature. I Corinthians 3:1-2, Hebrews 5:12-13. God desires that we grow to become mature disciples. We exercise our own freedom and choose our own path. God continues to love us when our choices are bad.

Changes are ahead for all of us. Reflect on the changes that have already happened. Ephesians 2:10. We are God's workmanship. To make decisions for God, we choose to discover ourselves.

We will learn the will of God. Circumstances do not determine whether we are inside or outside God's will. Decisions are complicated and have unexpected results.

Decisions that are made with a Christ-centered mind. If that is true of our decisions, all of creation stands on tiptoe to see the sons and daughters of God coming into their own.

Christ-Centered Decision Making and Risk

Faith is not only a means of obeying, but an act of obedience to God. It is not just an altar on which to sacrifice, but it is a sacrifice itself. Living faith is a process. The grace of God leads to faith in God. Faith results in good works. Hebrews 11. As with all my previous books, this one is my effort to speak to the deepest needs and concerns of people today. My commitment to listen to people and then to God as God speaks through the Scriptures is reflected in the content of this writing. Faith requires risk. God asks us to be willing to risk. The greater the risk, the greater the faith given.

Nothing has brought me more joy than to be a small part in seeing people respond in churches all around the world. I pray that there is "a sweet, sweet spirit in this place" wherever you worship.

My personal vision quest is to live life more fully and to be practical and personal in what I have preached and written. I pray that my readers will be renewed in their faith and their faithfulness.

Jim, I know you feel waters rising as you and your wife Laurel deal with so many medical issues. I know how you feel helpless. You cannot stop the rain from falling or life waters from rising.

I understand how the current is strong and your bodies are tired. You feel so empty for your accomplishments and worldly possessions are floating away. They appear to be floating away.

I shall give you, My strength. I know you grieve them going on downstream. I hear you when you realize your patience is drowning with your shaken faith

I will help you think as I think. My ways are not your ways. I will guide you from My perspective, as all your losses will be replaced.

Focus on your blessings, family and friends, faith and mercy. I am there with you when the waters rise around you in your soul, even though your faith and hope have been swept downstream.

Remember how I got you through your past floods. You were never meant to make it alone. Blessings will be released as you pray to me. My desire is for my children to identify our family likeness as brothers and sisters in my eternal family. Your faithing prayers must be implemented by getting with people and their struggles.

Seek my guidance for learning whom I have placed on your agenda and what I mean in my loving kindness. I will give you fresh grace to live each day. You cannot live on yesterday's inspiration. It is my desire that you relinquish your fears and frustrations, problems, and hurts.

My challenge to you is to live as if this was your last day of living on the earth. Live it to the fullest. I will speak to you if you will just be still. Listen to me. Be silent and let me help you. I will tell you the way to go forward.

Time and memory will fade. I am the same yesterday, today, and tomorrow.

Chapter One

FAITH AND FAITHFULNESS

Our faith is the cornerstone of our spiritual lives. Without it, we are lost at sea. We are vulnerable to every changing tide and strong current. The Bible tells us that the Lord is close to the faithful, no matter what. Jesus told us many things about the power of faith. Mark 11:22-23. Faith can move mountains, part seas, and set us free. Faith overwhelms us with God's reality. A small child surrounded by strangers in a crowded place might be overwhelmed with fear. A woman who has lost her husband to cancer is overwhelmed by grief. Setting our minds and souls on the things of God we are overwhelmed by grace and love. Set your eyes on God, not on troubles. Psalm 144:7, 11.

Faithfulness begins with God. Psalm 36:5. When we fly in an airplane, we take off. We get higher and higher. There comes a point when we break through the clouds. In that moment, we see an open blue sky. We are now looking down on the clouds.

Thousands of years ago, in ancient Israel, the clouds appeared to be ridiculously high and beyond the reach of humans. The psalmist likened the reach of the faithfulness of God to reaching beyond the clouds. Ur God of faithfulness is faithful in the areas of covenant, the Word, trustworthiness and fruitfulness. Psalm 119:75. Trustworthiness results from faithfulness.

Search for scriptural levels of trust. II Kings 12:13-15. Do you want to be trusted? Be faithful in all your encounters. Be faithful in how you handle our money. Be faithful in your commitments. Turn up when you say you will. Do what you say you will do.

Be faithful in prayer. Be faithful in reading the Word of God. There are rewards for faithfulness. There is punishment for unfaithfulness. Faithfulness is part of the fruit that God produces.

When I was studying at Cardiff Theological College in London, I heard the story of Charles Spurgeon's grandfather named James. James had a large family and very little money was coming in. He loved the Lord and was faithful.

Spurgeon's family had a cow. They needed it to provide milk for their children. One day the cow died. Spurgeon's wife was filled with concern and anxiety.

Spurgeon said to his wife, "God said God would provide. It is possible that God could send us fifty cows." Each day in London, a group of pastors in a covenant group met to help poorer pastors. They shared a pot of money to give to pastors who were in need. They doled out what they had had, and they had five pounds left. They decided to send it to James Spurgeon. Each pastor placed more money and now had twenty pounds. That was a lot in those days. God was always faithful. And in the grace, love, and joy, we must be faithful too.

God has no lack, the source of all beings and existence. Psalm 46:1, 7. We are overwhelmed by undeserved love. In the times of darkness, turmoil, and inadequacy, we can hold on to experience an overwhelming nearness to God.

God is unmovable security, a towering shelter. We are surprisingly overwhelmed. Human beings are like a mere breath. She is like a passing shadow. We are overwhelmed by the glory and splendor of God.

Being overwhelmed by God moves us to be confident, dependent, and intimate in our prayers. God is our salvation. We find a new song in our hearts. Being overwhelmed by God rings us into prayer, not in paralysis, but with desperate boldness. The truth of God's character floods our thoughts.

Look at your life. If your faith is active with faithfulness, you will naturally reflect Christ. Going deep into intimacy with God, you will live each moment guidance. James 2:17. In our initial leap of faith is simply believing that all God said was true. God continually tells us we are to move with faith.

Mother Teresa said, "Faith in action is love, and love in action is service. By transforming that faith into living acts of love, we put ourselves in contact with God and with Jesus our Lord."

Walking by faith and not by sight is a scary journey, especially when our exceptions for the ending result are different from God. Waking by faith means that we bring ourselves into alignment with God, not the other way around. When we run our race, we require faith. Philippians 3:14.

Strong faith leads us toward our hopes. James 2:26. Our actions are needed to please God. Faithfulness stirs us on to be like Jesus Christ. Faith means we do what we are able to love. To share. To be generous. To point people to Jesus. Our actions seem small. Mustard-seed faith is enough.

To step out in faith takes trust and courage. Getting out of our comfort zone is part of living in grace and love. Step one brings an aura of excitement and joy. We will never be completely prepared God never asks us to be ready to go. God just tells us to go. We will be getting ready along the faithful way.

The fruitful reality of faith, the act of faithfulness puts us in contact with God. Faith opens us little by little to all the treasures and mysteries of God. Faith is the light that never deceives us. Lack of faith is the heart of sin. It is quite difficult and hard to confront. Lean on God with full trust.

Jesus insists on the importance of faith. What Jesus chides his disciples for is not their human weaknesses, but for their lack of faith. Matthew 17:20, Luke 17:6. God has used the power through more than a million written and published books. John 20:30-31.

Faith is active in the present moment. Faithfulness is not putting things off. II Corinthians 6:2. After death we don't need faith. In heaven, the time for faith will have passed. God respects our dignity, our free will. For eternity, we shall have what we loved and placed our faith during our adventure on earth. Reflect on the times when you lacked faith. Ask Jesus to help us to keep growing in faith. Faith is a gift from grace and human decision.

God gives the gift of faith. I Corinthians 12:9. Even in the times when what we are being asked to do appears impossible, faith enables us to leap. God is full of surprises. Your leap of faith involves not just you alone God is with you.

Faithful souls enter into the rest of God. Hebrews 4:11. Faith rests. Faithfulness leans on our beloved. My daughter, sound asleep, often slept on my shoulder no matter what sounds were around her. That is rest. That is faith. A child's trust in her father is so complete that she can abandon herself to his will, believing she will be safe.

We can rest in the will of God. God is our refuge in every storm. We need not worry. Only God brings the fulfillment of rest. Faith is not foolhardiness. It is not putting ourselves into harm's way, expecting God to pull us out. Faith is the casual confidence. Faith is a toddler or an infant sleeping on her father's shoulder.

Faith is belief, assurance of God's word, love, joy, grace and gentleness and the fruit of the Spirit. Faithfulness is living in accord with faith. Faith leads to faithfulness. Faithfulness does not save. It reflects God's faithfulness.

God is able to work with us. When we work, God rests. When we rest, God works. What are barriers to doing something every day that requires faith? Overcoming those barriers can be accomplished with our mustard seed faith.

With the gift of faith, we see the world through the eyes of Christ. Christ's way of seeing in not surface sight. We see beneath as the hand of God leads us through the maze of life. In faith we experience the love and grace of God. We need a life of faith because every in our spiritual life comes from faith. Galatians 2:20.

Faith is given by God to fulfill the Creator's purpose. In the end of days, God is glorified. Faith provides answers for our needs. We must gain a revelation of the will of God for specific purposes. Praying for healing is to focus on the will of God. Healing does not depend on us.

All things are possible with God. Fervent prayer brings into existence that which God has spoken. James 5:16. The disciples asked Jesus how to pray. Luke 11:5-8. We must operate in faith according to God's timetable not ours.

Hebrews 11:2 tells us that by a faith that produces faithfulness the ancient men and women obtained a good report. Their faith led to faithful conduct that testified to the reality of their faith.

We are puzzled by the names of those who received a faithful report. If only faultless people were listed, the account provides little in the way of encouragement for ordinary people such as you and me.

They were faithful, but were they faithful until the end? Being faithful for a time or for today may be easy. Marriages often begin well, but half of them will not end well. Many start a job well, but do not end well. Many begin a life race, but they will never finish. Our desire and intention is to remain faithful to the end.

Dear reader, God is telling us that the faithful who came before will not proceed those who came afterward. Just as they were faithful to the end, and will receive the promise, the inheritance of an eternal glory, we can also be faithful to the end and receive the promise from God, our Creator. Paul writes about being faithful in his second letter to the Corinthians. The apostle is reaching out to the church he founded, but it has since rejected him. Faith has been shaken. Paul wants to reconcile with the congregation. The apostle has been in prison. He says he hopes to visit them again.

Paul trusted a believer named Tychicus. Tychicus was fully trusted to be the person to deliver Paul's letters with hundreds of miles on a perilous journey. In the apostle's letter to Christians in the Ephesian congregation, he writes about Tychicus, his close friend and partner in ministry. Paul trusted him to publish his insights on his views on faithfulness. Ephesians 6:21-22.

When most people use the word faithful, our attention is drawn to the context of marital fidelity. Using "faithful" in this way is biblically accurate. Paul's use of the word illustrates the life of Tychicus. In Holy Scripture, faithfulness is a fruit of the Holy Spirit. Galatians 5:22-23.

Partners in Ministry

Faithfulness is to be continually accomplished with our ministry partners. It is a requisite, an indispensable characteristic, for those who have intimate communion with God.

Paul was writing his letters from prison in Rome as indicated in Ephesians 6:20. That was his writing office for his letters to not only Ephesians, but Colossians, Philippians, and Philemon. Colossians 4:7-9. Paul is not able to go to them because of his imprisonment. Tychicus became Paul's emissary to these churches. Philippians 1:12. Paul's difficult circumstances serves as an illustration of his ability to trust a fellow worker for Christ who had proved to be faithful. Paul's friend was called a" beloved brother and faithful servant of the Lord."

Tychicus is first mentioned in scripture in Acts 20:4. He was Asian and was chosen by Paul to take the relief offering to Jerusalem. This was the beginning of a mutually caring relationship. Tychicus was available and teachable.

Collegiality is a natural feature of faithfulness. In the world of ministry, Paul did not make people refer to him with hierarchical superiority. The most effective word "brother" refers to bishops, area denominational leaders, missionaries, and teachers. These are privileged positions, but they are held by ordinary human beings. He never sat up front in the churches he had founded, as if he was above those to whom he ministered.

Motivation in work and ministry are enhanced when followers sense shared ownership. We need strategic partners in the gospel to achieve our God-given callings. Paul believed others are teammates and partners.

Tychicus was counted on to complete the smallest tasks or the most difficult. Paul's humble leadership created faithful self-starters, self-sufficient for doing the ministry.

The real key to fulfillment of the Great Commission is to show grace with one another. We are so blessed by what we have seen God do through partnerships. We look to others to enable us to accomplish miracles. These brothers and sisters enable us to touch the world.

Those who have the fruit of faithfulness share their Christlikeness. If we are to become like Jesus means, we must be faithful to him and other people. I Thessalonians 5:24, II Thessalonians 3:3.

Too many believers are faithful only to the degree it is advantageous to themselves. True believers are faithful even when it costs you something to remain faithful.

Faithfulness is developed and cultivated throughout our brief journey in this world. Psalm 78:8, Luke 16:10. It is normal for us to want to be compensated for our work. There is a connection between faithfulness and reward. Proverbs 28:20, Nehemiah 7:2, Luke 12:42, I Timothy 1:12, II Timothy 2:2. God rewards faithfulness.

We, like Tychicus and those whom we trust, were faithful to God and others. God will strengthen and bless and deem us faithful. May that we said of all of us reading this book.
Your faithfulness will give you joy as we share the Word of God throughout the world.

Paul writes about his struggles. He says that he has worked faithfully for God. He has been in prison numerous times. He was beaten more times than he can count. Five times he was beaten with whips. Three times the Romans used rods. He was even stoned, but he survived. He had experience being shipwrecked. In his travels, he faced dangers from rivers, dangers from robbers, and dangers from his own people. Dangers also came from foreigners, in cities and in the countryside, and when he was sailing on the seas.

His faith had been shaken at every turn. He must have wondered if it was worth it. Going back to his old life was better than what kind of living he has now. For the apostle, the brutality which he suffered at the hands of the Romans, Jewish authorities, and the rejection of his own community of believers in Corinth. These were not indications of Paul's unfaithfulness. Faith is both a gift and fruit of the Spirit. Mark 4:28. Faith is received like a mustard seed. Matthew 13:31-32, 17:20. We do not want to live the rest of our lives with only a small seed of faith. We want our faith to grow and mature. For righteousness to increase in our lives, faith must grow.

Faith must increase for us to become better partakers of the imparted righteousness of God, so we fully reflect the image and nature of Christ. When we continue to show our faithfulness to fellow believers and those with home we share our faith in Christ, there will be celebrations of eternal joy starting today.

Faith as the Human Response to Share Eternal Life

The human response to the revelation of God in Christ Jesus is faith. Humans are helpless. Faith is to continue relying on God. Sharing the life of God is faith. Sharing God's thinking is faith. We synchronize our thoughts with the thoughts of God. Faithfulness causes a unity with God's thinking. We share eternal life.

Jesus answered the question about faithfulness by beautifully modeling the characteristics of faith. Hebrews 3:1. Scripture tells us what happens when we live in the ways of God. God brings gifts into our lives, the same way that God brings gifts into our lives like fruit in an orchard.

When we embrace the fruit of faithfulness, we learn to be faithful to God, to ourselves, and to others. I Corinthians 13:7. Faithfulness results in steadfast love. God's steadfast love is extremely powerful. Human love is only a fraction of the steadfast love that Christ gives us. Proverbs 3:3-4.

Faith comes alive, sometimes suddenly, by the simple touch of a caring person. Faithfulness means not only speaking words, but with our works. We act as Jesus would act. If there is a gap between what we say and how we act, faith becomes stagnant. Our body language speaks without words.

God is present in any action, work, and relationship. Faith brings peace with each breath we take.

Faithfulness requires acceptance and patience. Lack of patience gets in the way. Impatience leads to discouragement. Scripture tells us how God acts in history. Romans 12:12. Faithfulness requires commitment.

Biblical faith weaves together stories from the Bible to point us to life for which we are called. Biblical faith gives insights into the joyful moments of life. Biblical stories cause changes in us. (Ken Harrison, *A Daring Faith in a Cowardly World: Live a Life Without Waste, Regret, or Anything Unfinished, pp. 4-22)*

I have enjoyed visiting and preaching in the provinces of Canada. The name of one of the denominations where I have standing is the Christian Church (Disciples of Christ) in the United States and Canada.

When you travel from Nova Scotia to Newfoundland, you must place your automobile or truck onto a huge cargo ship. Canada has more water than any other nation in the world. People sleep on the cargo ship. Most trips are perfectly safe. At quite rare trips, something may happen. Some of my Canadian friends told me about an old Toyota truck that slipped from the edge of the ship and submerged in shallow water. They shared about the tremendous effort and ingenuity to pull it out. When the driver started the engine, the truck was able to move again. Faith is the quality of being reliable to someone or something. Like that old Toyota truck, faith is being trustworthy and dependable.

The purpose of this book is to draw close to the reality of our existence and our life journey. Every moment is a meeting with God who loves us. Faith is a way of seeing. By God's grace, faith leads us through the maze of life.

Faithfulness leads us on

My deepest desire is to bear fruit for God. I want to be like a chokecherry tree. These trees flourish with a heavenly fragrance that draws people as Jesus did. Chokecherry trees produce abundant fruit that is a source of nourishment. My faith desires are to see families of the world flourishing, souls saved for heaven by grace and love, and the advance of the kingdom of God.

Remaining faithful may be perceived as impossible, but it is a challenge worth pursuing. We must continually reexamine our faith. Introspection is necessary. Keep praying and continue journaling. During the storms of life in the dark times, we feel like an uprooted sapling. Instead of flourishing, we become dry and bear no fruit. Our zeal is gone.

The cares of this world pull us away, exhausts our strength. Our faith has become a little faith. I Timothy 6:20-21. Paul writes that we must be faithful to spread the gospel. People declare that they are committed but they never help spread it. There is no passion for missions. We must be faithful to the biblical truths about personal witnessing.

Stay focused. Christians will face temptation to follow false teachings. Paul is warning us to be faithful to the Word of God. Listen to these warnings not to wander. I Timothy 6: 21.

Signs of wander include a lack of love for scripture. There is less attention given to reading the Bible. We can ask the Holy Spirit to give us understanding and direction.

Wandering means less love for the children of God. Our fellowship grows cold. We spend less and less time with fellow believers. This is another clear warning. I Corinthians 12:12-13.

There is a decline in prayer. Intimate faith with God is not felt with a lack of devotion to God. Prayer is the believer's power supply. We are then gradually finding changes in our thinking. We begin to change our convictions.

Everybody feels disconnected from faith. We can open our Bibles to find inspiration. Biblical figures struggled to recognize their beliefs in the doubts and hostility. Moses, who witnessed the Lord within a burning bush, questioned whether his people would believe his testimony. Moses led his people to safety. We are also inspired by the biblical stories of Job, Noah, Jeremiah, Esther, and Mary.

Jesus is the ultimate inspiration. Christ was rejected, despised, and ultimately killed. Abide in Jesus. Without him we are torn from our union with God, who makes us fruitful.

N.T. Wright noted, "Faith and obedience are not antithetical. The belong exactly together. Indeed, the word faith can be translated as faithfulness." Many English translations have "faith in Christ" or "faith in Jesus Christ." Romans 3:22, 26, Galatians 2:16, Philippians 3:9. Christ is the object of faith. At the level of grammar, the Greek expression that has no prepositions and can be read either way. Therefore, Saint Paul writing "faith," is their "faithfulness." Humans must place their faith in Christ. The righteous of God comes by "faith in Christ," or "the faithfulness of Christ." (D.A. Carson, *A Life of Faith and Forgiveness*, pp. 97-103)

Sharing in the life of God makes us "new persons." We comprehend reality both temporal and eternal. We touch God. Difficulties in spiritual life stem from our weak faith. Faith shares in God's thinking. To have faith is synchronizing our thought with divine thought. Faithfulness is having the mind of Christ.

Unfaithfulness Is Friendship with the World

To be spiritually unfaithful is the result of our friendship with the world. James 4:4-5. Committing spiritual adultery is to profess to have Christian faith, but to attempt to find pleasure and captivation in the worldly influence, financial security, comforts and wild choices. I John 2:15-16.

Spiritual unfaithfulness is like trying to staddle a fence. "Lukewarm" is a biblical word for this. Revelation 3:15-16.

In our culture infidelity is unfaithfulness to a spouse or sexual partner. It changes the foundation between two people forever. Being faithful during marriage is only as strong ss the people who make their vows.

Maintaining a bond with a spouse is essential. Problems come from spending extra time with colleagues and friends, fellow workers. Calling outside of work, sending emails, or flirting leads to faithless emotional attachments. Adultery is forgivable. It is not, as some say, unpardonable. God's mercy, change of behavior, and soul-searching brings peace.

Forgiveness is for everyone. Repentance involves spiritual and physical effort that reaches every corner of our lives. It leaves no secrets. By accepting the love and grace of God, our burdens are lifted. This means that any sin we commit, including infidelity, is forgiven when we come to Jesus with a repentant heart.

Forgiveness does not exempt us from the consequences of our actions. Sexual sins scare us deeply. We need an extra portion of the grace God freely gives.

Jesus is the perfect image of God. Hebrews 1:3. The hymn, "Great Is Thy Faithfulness," Whatever the season, "summer and winter, springtime and harvest," or whatever the struggle, "pardon for sin, and a peace that endureth," God faithfully acts.

When the storms of life come, we must cling to Christ. Faith discovers the life of God in creation. Faithing perceives the will of God in phenomena that sees events as signs of God's presence.

The more we infuse prayer into our life routine, the more connected we will be to faith. Praying feels intimidating. Instead of striving to deliver an eloquent prayer, incorporate short, simple prayers. Our persistence will ultimately do wonders in our faithfulness.

By faith, Christ becomes a light which shines through a person's life journey. Divine will comes as a gift in grace. Grace is an expression of love. Every experience is linked to the love of God who loves us.

Faithfulness is a higher virtue than effectiveness. Faith reaches a point, regardless of what others think or do, the faithful said no. Faithfulness was higher than effectiveness. The faithful are remembered more than the effective. Remembrance results because they placed their lives completely in the hands of God. They accomplished the will of God. They bore a faithful life, that brought the unexpected and miraculous result of a concrete witness to Jesus.

God's grace is made perfect in weakness. Our bodies are living sacrifices, acceptable to God. God expects us to remain faithful. Hebrews 12:1-2. (George Hunsinger. "From a Great Cloud of Witnesses," *Weavings: A Journal of the Christian Spiritual Life*, II, 2, pp. 26-29.

Effectiveness is, only by the grace, love, joy of God. In the end, we will not have lived in vain.

The Creator guides everything with eternal wisdom. Faith is security and peace. Faith brings confidence of always being immersed in the love of God. In a church of the spirit of joy, the tone of the community is compassionate. He community understands that the struggle against sin and corruption is difficult. Sin is taken seriously. The community of faith feels safe. The focus is on Jesus the Christ crucified. The sacraments are the signs of God's faithfulness to us, not our faithfulness to God.

Being Immersed in the Love of God

When I was writing the first draft of this book, it was erased by Microsoft Word. It simply devastated me. I lost ideas and notes for four books planned in 2023, all my financial records, so much that shot into my soul. This obvious sign of attachment was also my sadness as God took something away from me. Only after agonizing prayer, did I accept in joy these situations. Only then could I submit with serenity that God was freeing me. Matthew 6:33.

Faith creates within us a tension as we continuously revolve our lives around our will. Our will involves what is convenient. It does not fit what God wants. We are so defensive about our desires which are self-seeking. God foils our plans so we can unite with the will of God.

Faithfulness Is Total Trust

Faithing is to rely on nothing apart from God. God watches with admiration the miracle of human faith, especially child-like faith, which expresses itself in giving up everything. This is a total entrusting.

Seek grace. That is Paul's understanding of the faithful life. Grace is a good description of the work of God's mercy toward undeserving sinners such as us. Paul gives this passionate plea for Timothy, and to all believers to be faithful.

Jesus' mother Mary is an example of God's power overriding human efforts. Luke 1:35. Mary was shocked and when Gabriel made a sudden appearance telling Mary of her unique mission. Luke 1:30-34. The angel empowered Mary to ask questions with her faith. Her unwavering faithfulness brought her a visit from a messenger of God. Luke 1:26-29.

Mary trusted God so completely, she asked what God's mysterious salutation meant. Mary's faith inspires us to desire to know and love God so deeply that we trust faithfully in sudden encounters.

Mary brought Jesus into the world through the power of the Holy Spirit. Everything Mary did was a testimony to the love of God. She demonstrated what faith is.

During the storms of life, our support crumbles away. Grace is attached to this truth. God in Christ expects us to entrust in Jesus. Jesus came as a child, an infant, who depended on the care of adults. He was stripped of everything.

Whatever the situation, we should remember not to worry. Remember the love and faithfulness of God. Proverbs 3:5-6, First Corinthians 15:57, Second Corinthians 2:14-16, First Thessalonians 5:16-18.

In losing my computer materials, I reacted to a situation, rather than trusting God. Hebrews 12:2-3. If we wait on the Lord, our strength will be renewed. Isaiah 40:31. As we learn to trust our Lord, and not run after our own understanding, we will gain a new spiritual perspective.

Not a human on earth is perfect. We will fail. We will face difficult situations. We will doubt God. We will experience God's faithfulness as we look back. Growing up, we are aware that opening and closing doors is part of God's faithfulness.

When Paul wrote instructions to young pastor Timothy, he told him to be an example to his church. I Timothy 4:12. Some people look down on youth. I experience this as I began preaching at the tender age of 12. Of course, it happens now as a retired 80-year-old minister.

We must have faith to be faithful. We can't have faith without displaying faithfulness. Deepest faith leads to faithful Christ-centered living. Timothy and ministers today are not perfect, but they are to be examples of faith and faithfulness.

Strong inner faith is evidence of the outward working of faith. Timothy was younger than most members of his church, still he had this awesome responsibility. We are tempted to believe that faithfulness is best proven in grand, public ways. God commends faithfulness in the little things. We could be invited to be faithful in bigger things. Luke 16:10.

We should not waste our time longing and waiting for large opportunities that never come to most people. Every gathering in every church should react to the spirit and the prayers of God's people.

God can transform the people who worship in any size congregation. No wonder those who have felt the Lord's joy continue to stay and rejoice with those who have chosen to follow the way of Jesus.

Some Insightful Questions

Good journalists begin with basic questions: Where is faith? What is faith? Why do we have faith? Who has faith? How does faith develop?

Where is faith? Faith exists among people who are called to live according to the will of God. Faith is an external, objective reality in which we participate. We will become part of a faith-based community. Interactions with fellow believers energizes us and renews our commitment.

Faith is more about letting our light shine before others so that people may see our good deeds and glorify our Father in heaven. The whole world can be inspired by our faith-driven lifestyles. Faith traces the work of God in all things. Faith gives security and peace. We probably will face anxiety and become uneasy. Faithfulness develops faith. We find more strength as we struggle. Faithfulness develops fruit. We know the reality of God.

Our unfaithful world could use a heavy dose of compassion. Regardless of how people around us believe or behave, we demonstrate compassion for their life challenges. God has continually demonstrated compassion for us. Psalm 116:5.

Faith is inside us. Faithing organizes the character of life. Faith is far from beyond. Faith, love, and grace is authored and bestowed by God, received from God. It is a sacred trust. Our child-like faith performs miracles by common people. A faithful person oozes out faith as the Holy Spirit works within us.

What is faith? Faith holds firm to teachings. Faith feels its way to the Supreme Being as the faithful experience love from God and respond with their own love. Faith deals with what we do, than what we think or feel. As a licensed therapist, I have discovered that people with emotional problems are those stunted in faith.

Why do we have faith? Faith is a meaning-making activity. Faith is a means of relating to God. We have a God-shaped vacuum that only can be filled by God.

Who has faith? Those who have faith hold on to affirmations and certain realities. Tension comes with assumptions of who has faith. We will discuss this later in a chapter on conversion and faithfulness.

How does faith develop? Jesus' teaching about the mustard size faith is a foundation thought. Mature faith means more faith. Faith does not develop as human bodies or thinking patterns develop. Faith is a gift. Faith is like a caterpillar's growth into a butterfly. Faith shifts in function, appearance, and form.

Faith is openness to God. Faith is relational, a transformation. Faith is evolving and evolved. Life situations change us and bring on differing plans and unexpected burdens. God keeps calling on those who have eyes to see and ears to hear, to look and listen. We are saved by grace through faith. Proverbs 2:9-10.

God is only love and only good. Our Redeemer loves us boundlessly. God is always seeking souls to flood them with love. We cannot love our neighbors or other human beings without loving God. We must be fully open to Christ inside in which Christ can fully live and love. Opening ourselves through faith, Jesus becomes "the way, the truth, and the life." John 14:6.

Without Christ we can do nothing. Christ is our life. We allow Christ to love within us, and we allow Christ to live inside of our souls. Galatians 2:20. Christ has an unusual desire. He wants to love each of us with a suitable love. His desire is to have us see his face in a different way. We love and we grow in love.

This concept has differing meanings. We pass from young to old like the shift from water to ice. Our bodies will break down. We lose the ability to run a marathon. Her hair turns from blonde to gray. It is difficult to view ourselves positively in later years. (Connie Zweig, *The Inner Work of Age: Shifting from Role to Soul*, pp. 20-45)

Christ lives within us to the extent that we beckon him, as we see ourselves in weakness. We cannot undertake this unusually difficult call which requires heroism. Humility is required. God is ready to give everything to a person who credits nothing to themselves.

So much is expected of us. We are members of a privileged family. We are children of a King. Someday God will reward us for the things we do. The yardstick for faithfulness is how faithful we are with our own talents.

We can then re-image faithful possibilities. We are obliged to do something. Who am I if I do nothing?

The transformation we go through is profound, mostly invisible, slightly messy, and a continuing process. The pandemic, the deadly hurricane Ian, the fires in California, and the war in Ukraine causes a pause button for life. Life for millions in unrecognizable from what it was.

When we press play again, life will resume more or less like it did before these disasters. Our ministries have changed. No version of before makes any sense to return. Without our familiar guideposts, there are possibilities for new creations beyond those we have imagined.

We have been forced to a new faith transformation. Faithing is fearful and confusing. We read stories of struggles in transforming faithfulness. Other stories are of people resisting change. As a writer I enjoy these stories.

Personal transformation is difficult because we expect it to be hard. Faith is intense so often. There is always a gap between where we are and the unknown where we are going in faith and our faithfulness as we are fully precent to the current moment and our uneasy world.

Do not be discouraged. God's faithfulness will never waver. God continues to provide, comfort, support, and strengthen. Life has brought us things out of our control. Philippians 4:19.

God is faithful. God is love, compassionate, merciful. God's fidelity is a virtue of constancy, reliability, and goodness.

There is a correlation between goodness of faithfulness. Goodness is perfect through faithfulness. God initiates good things for us. Faith by grace gifts us with joyous bounties in our lives. Lamentations 3:22-23.

God always fulfills promises. Genesis 13:16. These transcend time and eras, guaranteeing future joy. Our Lord does not change. James 1:17. God never changes. God will bless us beyond our imaginations.

The theological word "omnipresent" is one description of God. Comfort in grief, help in darkness and difficulties, and shaken faith. Isaiah 41:10. Anxiety and worry are not necessary. God is with us everywhere, including your most difficult experiences.

God loves us all the time. Paul recognized this for himself. II Timothy 2:13.

No matter what mistakes and sins we have committed, we know that God does not rely on our human ability to be faithful.

Life Is Not Fair

Life is not fair. Still our essential needs are supplied. Darkness causes us to think that we will not survive. We must be more God dependent instead of being self-dependent. Philippians 1:6. Faith uplifts and encourages Each new day give us another opportunity to place our faithful trust in God.

We have nothing to fear as we wait for the fulfillment of the promises of God. This assurance is a fruit of the Spirit.

God comforts our spirits. God's comfort is beyond understanding. It provides rest and reassurance for our weary souls. Heaven brings us infinite joy. Joy is the connection to life that is bigger than us. Joy means touching heaven. Joy exists on a different plane than other human emotions. Joy is a sign of God inside us. We were created for experiencing joy as joy is the connection to heaven.

Life weighs us down. It knocks the wind out of our sails. Faithing makes living stronger in our weakness. We do not have to be ashamed of our weaknesses because grace gives us strength. The faithful are vulnerable.

During the times when we feel inadequate, that we are not enough, we have the chance to share the good news of God's strength.

We can depend on a community of support. When we feel that nobody understands us, God will provide support for us. Hebrews 10:25.

Like Jesus' disciples we struggle because of our "little faith. We follow our perceptions rather than the faith in God. Faith is not a" belief without proof." Faith is not belief without proof despite the evidence.

Faith is complete trust in someone or something. Christianity is faith-based. It is faith in the person and work of Jesus Christ. Lacking this perception, our lives do not reflect that we believe what we claim to believe.

This world distracts us. By "this world," we mean the accepted wisdom of this world and the faithless culture that surrounds us. The faithless are out of favor, lacking passion and fervor. In the Hebrew Scriptures, removal from the Promised Land showed God's displeasure and a consequence of unfaithfulness. Deuteronomy 28:36-44. God feels distant. The fire once felt is snuffed out. It is not a matter of just having more faith.

We must be constantly reminded of what Christ has done for us. Romans 10:17. Faith is built up as we continually hear the gospel preached. God knows that the spirit is willing, but the flesh is weak. Mark 14:38.

God Ignites a Fresh Fire

God steps into our unfaithful ordinary world as the extraordinary healer. God seeks to ignite a fresh fire. It is possible to renew and to feel renewed joy in our relationship with God.

If life is rough now, a little faith inside will yearn to trust God. The fear of God seems as untrustworthy, unpredictable, and unreliable. As life tends to let us down, we can always ask God for help. Trusting God with our shattered lives is difficult. Simply trusting, even with doubts and a tiny slither of faith can make possible is trust.

Marel von Ostendorf researched the value of faith and faithfulness. Definitions of faith and faithfulness have evolved. (Marel von Ostendorf, *The Theory of Faithfulness*, pp. 34-45)

Faithfulness sustains relationships without salient propositions. The faithfulness of God is beyond our understanding. God is faithful in times when we are not.

Synchronistic Theological Understanding

My theological understanding is synchronistic. Some days I find comfort in Calvinism. Other days I see God's sovereignty in Arminianism. I have shared the joy of the Lord in regard to our depravity because of our sin. They think that they must trust God with divine assistance provided to everybody. Calvinists think ordinary people are unable to trust God without grace to change their minds toward believing.

Calvinism says we are chosen. God chooses who will be mercifully brought to faith. Arminianism also believes we are chosen. All of us have been elected to salvation.

Both doctrines hold that in the death of Christ, God provided sufficient atonement for all creatures. Arminianism believes salvation is effective by faith. Calvinists believes salvation is only for the elect. They believe being born again is the work of God, of renewal of our hearts, bringing saving faith.

Calvinists teach that God works to preserve us in the faith. No one is ever lost as they are born of the spirit of God. Arminianism also believes that God works to preserve us in faith and faithfulness, but that we can fall away from grace.

Both doctrines concern how humans can be saved. Calvinists believe that God has to produce in us the desire for Christ. Arminianism say we must express this desire for Christ.

I am not a Calvinist, nor am I Arminian. These are just theological systems conceived by fallible men. I am deeply and eternally grateful to God who loved me, a sinner, so much. I reject the idea that I received salvation on any merit of my own. Ephesians 2:8-9.

We have no righteousness or goodness upon which to base our salvation. Romans 3:23, 5:8. One of the members of the Two-Seed-in-the-Spirit Predestinarian Baptist Church said, "She was not ever going to have children because she was afraid God would not elect them to salvation.

Many in Christian history have fallen into the trap of going further that the Bible goes and with human rationalization, try to systemize the actions of God. This ends in extremism. It is extreme to God has elected some to be damned to hell and does not offer salvation to them. It is also extreme to say that humans in any way merit salvation or lose eternal life that God gives as a gift to the believer. (Earle E. Cairns, *Christianity Through the Centuries*, p. 351)

I refuse to place God in a box to systemize God's act of saving the sinner. Extreme Calvinism casts a shadow over the assurance of salvation. The wonder if they have been elected or rejected, or if they have a choice to follow Christ. Calvinists declare that we have the inability to call upon Christ. If we are not one of the elect, we will not be saved.

During my 70 years as a minister, I have served Presbyterian and Methodist congregations. I also once preached in a Two-Seed-in-the-Spirit Predestinarian Baptist Church in the Great Smokey Mountains of East Tennessee. Nobody understands how the grace, love, and joy of God in Christ becomes eternally true for us.

In our faith journey, we think about Thomas, the disciple. When Thomas heard the stories of the resurrection, he refused to believe them until he saw Jesus with his two eyes. Jesus accommodated Thomas and his lack of faith by making an appearance to him. Jesus allowed him to touch and see the wounds.

Many today echo Thomas' experience saying unless I see Jesus face to face, I will not believe." We must not believe as unbelievers do. We must continue to walk by faith rather than by sight. Hebrews 11:6.

Doubt is a common, natural, and universal experience. Questioning does not lead us to shame and guilt. Temptations to sin may rise during dark times of doubt. Still doubting is not sinning.

Faithfulness Brings the Light of Christ

Cling to faith. Hold on to the Light. Faith causes our fears to take flight. Faith cannot be conjured up. Faith comes from the work of God. God quenches darkness and no soul is beyond reach. Living in faithfulness, Christ becomes a light that shines for our lifetimes. Faith is a gift. Faith is listed as part of the fruit in the Spirit. I Corinthians 12:7-11, Galatians 5:22-23.

The gift of faith is linked to the gifts of healing and the work of miracles. Faith is the basis for the operations of the Holy Spirit. That is why the gifts are so important.

Faith overrides natural laws. Faith makes the impossible possible. There is tremendous power in faith. Faith creates things that were not there before.

The gift of faith in particular is given when there are impossible obstacles that God wants to overcome. These are within the will of God. Faith produces. Where there is nothing, faith creates. Where there is no way, faith makes a way.

We must view everything with a heavenly view, knowing that nothing is able to stand before the awesome presence of God. There are no boundaries that faith cannot cross.

If we have faith flowing and working mightily within our lives, then there is no limit to what ordinary people such as us can accomplish wit and in the kingdom of God. Let us receive from the Author and Finisher of our faith all that is awaiting us in these days.

There is a tomorrow. There is exciting life. Faith insures that we shall walk in glory with loved ones who have entered into heaven.

It is always my prayer that we would serve God faithfully in this life so that we might all hear God say, "Well done, good and faithful servant." We are raised up to live with a loving, forgiving God in heaven eternally.

God has ordained with infinite wisdom that the faithful ones of all ages, whether they are young or old, male or female, tall or short, educated or uneducated, rich or poor, will enter heaven together.

Faithfulness and the Future of the Church

The most casual observer of faith in the United States face significant challenges that have undermined everything from their capacity to communicate with authority. They can't command loyalty from their own members.

There is little hope that the situation will change. There will be inexorable decline. We must resign ourselves to retreat into oblivion, continuing the embarrassing chaos of the past thirty years.

What have we now created? The problems have caused traditional Christianity to be in this moment. Hypocrisy and moral corruption abound in the eyes of the public. Clergy act like salespeople to attract and keep people in the church.

Technology has played a role. When the automobile was invented, some said with transportation, people would flock into the church. However, now it has been proven that roads run both ways. Cars allow individuals easy access to a greater range of churches. The internet has abolished geography. A person in California and listen to worship in a church in Germany that is on the web. Millions now worship online. Returning congregations after the covid epidemic have diminished or closed as a result.

The church is not something to be desired, but the New Testament teaches that church is not a part of the wider culture. The message of the cross is foolishness to the Greeks and an offense against the Jews.

The apostle Peter noted that Christians, in the world but not of it. We are sojourners and exiles. Politics has been psychologized in response to the rise of the therapeutic self for whom inner feelings are central to well-being. Combine this with the rise of social media, all of life is now performed in public.

We have created a world that has erased the boundary between private and public. This new situation makes personal religious convictions a mater o heated public interest. If we try to hold the traditional view of issues, we will run afoul of one of the terms of recognition in secular society. Many Christians beliefs are labeled as bigotry. Difficult choices must be made in the decade ahead.

Obviously, the church will become smaller and smaller. This wider social context already severely restricts the possibility of the church gaining credibility. Christian teaching is difficult to accept or to even imagine.

Jesus himself said love is the key when he taught that the love Christians have for each other would be the way people would know them as his disciples. In our society, love has little meaningful content in the wider culture. Church needs to be known as a community that cares for its own and extend this care to those outside.

This will look different in differing places. Community life in rural areas or a small village is inevitably not the same as that in an urban setting. Each congregation finds a way to be a loving community in the context in which it finds itself.

Communities offer places to belong. They shape our intuitive understanding of the world and our place within it. In our era, traditional communities are breaking down, people are feeling anxiety and distance from others.

It would be unfortunate if lamentation were the only response we have to the marginalization of the church. The church will always be in exile. The church is more than an institution that maintains a creed, more than a loving and nurturing community. Church is a worshipping body. Worship grips the whole person and the whole congregation. Liturgical actions include proclamation and response, prayer and confession, words and music, sacraments are all part of the joyful congregation. Worship transforms us. The joy of the Lord is real strength rather like the love of a community cannot be mediated by a computer screen.

Corporate singing in worship is of critical importance. The believer acts freely, singing the words and following the tune as an individual, intentional action. Singing, the community becomes a whole, and they lose their individual identity. Individual freedom and corporate belonging are tied together without tension or difficulty.

Believers find their true identity through participation in the corporate act of worship, addressed by God as part of God's people.

Accepting that faith and faithfulness will inevitably place the church at even more rejected by the society. The biblical promise is that the gates of hell shall not prevail against it. Faithful believers will forever hold on to this truth. Hebrews 10:23-29. The "assembling of ourselves together" in Hebrews 10:25 is a reference to the New Testament church of which every member is to be a faithful believer.

The Great Commission requires faithful workers, and those who neglect the church are neglecting responsible spiritual duty. No human institution can be successful apart from committed and faithful members. I Corinthians 4:2.

During the eras of the decline of the church, the first thing that fades is faithfulness to the assembly of the local church. Wavering believers become sporadic in attendance to their local congregation.

We can't remain strong in the faith without being faithful to the church. Powerful enemies will always be fighting against faith. Millions have shipwrecked because they became careless about their relationship to the church and its meetings.

Church is necessary for fellowship. I Timothy 3:15. Church is a spiritual family. Church is where we consider one another and help one another and teach one another and warn one another. The believer is not a spectator. The believer has a responsibility before God to be faithful to her church. Acts 2:42.

We believers need the preaching and teaching ministry of the leaders. Ephesians 4:11-14. She or he needs the ministry of singing Colossians 3:16.

It is a matter of spiritual safety. To neglect the assembly is spiritually dangerous. Every believer needs the church. It is the family of God. False religion both then and now attempts to replace the grace of God with something else. There is no joy of salvation in a perverted gospel. Romans 11:10.

FAITHFULLY LISTENING TO GOD

O James, I love that you are faithful to me. I want you to participate with My Spirit in your praying and your faithing. In grace, faithfulness is one of My gifts to you.

I will show you how to quiet physical desires, when you find them intense. Now dance with Me. I sense that you think you are missing something. I am not out there somewhere. I live in you and in your faith and faithfulness, you live in Me.

When I show you My great faithfulness, something happens in your body. Your heart skips even if your body stays still. If you are open to Me, your soul is infused with Me. We become one. We have become prayer, connected by My love, My joy, and our faithfulness.

I want you to rest in Me. It is difficult to rest in My busy world. In your private place, quiet your body and mind. I gave you imagination so you can come up with something unique.

Rest faithfully in Me each day, now, in the present time. Jim, child of Mine, bring your disappointments, rejections, and hurts to Me. Let Me continue to heal your soul. Let Me set you free.

Through your faith, you will come to understand My hidden plan. May you entwine My will with your will. I know your faith is dim now. Trust me. Your mind is not able to know the only and best way.

Focus on your joy, not the discontent. Don't cry for what you do not have. Count your blessing and share them again and again. I have given your patience and endurance. My marvelous grace helps you through temptations. I will give you wisdom to discern what is best for you.

Faith is the only thing that will hold you together when the world around us is falling apart. I want you to learn to live your life fueled by faith. There is nothing too big for Me to handle for you. My beloved, I am your God Who will move a mountain if it stands in the way of My will for you.

My power will be seen in your circumstance when you believe I am Who I say I am. You are Mine. I hold you in My hand. I love you, but I cannot force you to live by faith. I will never let you down or lead you astray.

I have a perfect plan for you if you will keep your eyes on Me. Jim, you have become like Me in many ways. Created in My image, I understand your inner most thoughts.

Jim, your church leaders, your publisher, your family have been facilitated by their faith and service. I have used their faithfulness and endurance to open the doors of heaven.

Chapter Two

FORGIVENESS AND FAITHFULNESS

Forgiving someone who has hurt us is quite difficult. We love to get revenge, to even the score. The bottom-line message of Jesus was to forgive. He wants us to love everybody. Salvation depends on God forgiving our sins. Faith transforms our lives. Relief arrives when we remember and are renewed in the joy in the assurance of eternal cleansing. Hebrews 9:14, I John 3:19.

Forgiveness is one of the most significant struggles Christians face. It is an integral aspect of faith. It is a goal every person of faith strives to achieve in all walks of life. In our struggles with sin, we must pray. Our heavenly Father is gracious, merciful, and long suffering. God invites us to become honest and open. Sin disrupts our fellowship with God. We must regularly need to be restored in the knowledge that we are forgiven.

My Greek professor at Carson-Newman University taught me the importance of understanding that the Greek word for "forgiven" tells us that this forgiveness is a completed action. The objective work of Christ Jesus secured the forgiveness of every trespassing, debts, and sin. I John 1:9.

Most of us struggle about the continuing sin in our lives. God tells us how to respond in faith. Romans 7. God provides ongoing help for those who have received forgiveness. God died for us while we were yet sinning.

Whenever our faith is shaken, it is easy to fall back to faulty thinking that our acceptance by God is performance-based. Stressing times lead to the resurrection of old addictions and struggles in our past.

Forgiveness is a central tenet of my faith. It is a gift from God who certainly could have held a grudge but did not. Forgiveness gives up any claims we might hold against others. Our futures are not bound by our past. Mark 11:25.

God's forgiveness is in unconditional love. It is for each one of us, no matter what we have done or have not done or have continued to do. If we desire to be more faithful to be a follower of Christ, to be a better spouse, to be a better friend, then I need to forgive.

The place of forgiveness cannot be overstated. In every relationship, offenses happen. Humans are not perfect. If we choose to forgive, we are not promised that we will feel better. It does lead to long-lasting contentment. The intentionality and effort are painful. Without forgiveness, a relationship will be broken or fractured. Unforgiveness causes premature death in a relationship. The spiritual art of forgiving maintains healthy relationships.

Forgiveness is a gift we give to ourselves and to those around us. Faithful people know the importance of forgiving. Embracing and choosing to forgive takes time. Forgiveness is a conscious decision to release feelings of resentment toward someone who has hurt us. Our transformed spirits release others. Ephesians 4:32.

Without forgiveness, we cannot avoid dysfunctional toxic relationships. We cannot walk in unforgiveness and show love and mercy. Soul care is not negotiable. Matthew 18:21-22, Hebrews 11:1-2.

Forgiveness is not forgetting. It does not excuse offences. It gives peace of mind. Unforgiveness erodes the fabric of our faith. It blocks our joy.

The movie *Unforgiven* stars Clint Eastwood, Gene Hackman, and Morgan Freeman gives a picture of unforgiveness bringing death. The film begins in Big Whisky, Wyoming where prostitutes offer reward money to anyone who will kill the cowboys who brutally murdered one of the girls named Delilah. Law enforcement thinks that she does not deserve justice.

It was Clintwood's best movie role. The film reminds us of Jesus' parable of the consequences of the unjust servant. The somber story in the film is a challenge to become endlessly forgiving. (Peter Malone and Rose Pacatte, *Lights, Camera, Faith: A Movie Lover's Guide to Scripture*, pp. 263-267) I have used this book in my preaching. There are hundreds of movies where a preacher can use to illustrate Scripture truths. I recommend it.

God had to leave heaven taking on human skin, a human face, and a human voice. Christ Jesus made it possible for any person to reach the vision of God. This visionary message as recorded in the New Testament is that we become one in the image of Jesus.

Forgiveness is difficult. We want to even the score and to obtain revenge. Forgiving makes us live more fully in the present time. We will never completely fail to remember the hurt. We do end the hate and plant love without revenge.

Germaine Saint Cloud wisely said, "Our sins do not cause God to love us less. No amount of good we do wins any greater love or forgiveness." Our capacity for memory must be filled with grace and gratitude to offset our failures. God heals memories. God knows we cannot grasp the present, or give ourselves to the future, until our past is expunged of any crippling memories. Forgiveness is the only way to the future freedom.

My wife Laurel and I have traveled to Germany many times. One trip took us to Wittenberg, the birthplace of the Reformation. We were wondering how Martin Luther managed to nail 95 theses to the bronze-solid door of the 500-year-old castle church.

Our tour guide informed us that that bronze door is a new addition. She noted that during the Seven Year's War, the original wooden door was lost in a fire that destroyed much of the church building in 1760. Most people know about the posting of the 95 theses, but few know the contents. Luther listed the abuses such as indulgences, the first one. He wrote: "When our Lord and Master, Jesus Christ said to repent, he called for the entire life of believers to be one of repentance. Luther's statement made public his teaching that repentance is not that easy, and one could pay for salvation. In the Lord's Prayer, we are taught to ask for forgiveness for all our past sins that the Holy Spirit brings to our memories, even the multitude of sins we cannot recall.

Justification Comes with Faith

The Word of God teaches that God requires faith and repentance to be justified. Faith and repentance are bound together. We review the process every day. We have been fully forgiven by God's grace.

Jesus taught about ending hate and planting love. "An eye for an eye" was not to be. Love our enemies and pray for those who hurt us. We must forgive others whatever harmful deeds they have done to us. If we did this, Jesus taught, we would overcome evil with good. Faithing is accepting his teachings when we understand that evil has the power of destroying us.

Forgiveness is vital. Forgiving ourselves and others is like watering parched land. Forgiveness softens and renews our spirit. We are all imperfect people. As an expression of our unreserved faith, we dare to risk the impossible.

Forgiveness is a choice that frees us to determine whether our relationship is able to move forward toward spiritual growth. This decision to forgive does not always feel good at the moment, however, it leads to long-lasting contentment.

Accepting the importance of forgiveness in a relationship takes intentionality and effort. That effort is painful. Without it, a relationship will be broken, stuck, and fractured. Forgiveness is the best way of maintaining healthy relationships.
Forgiveness will be the normal and natural. We shall become free and positive change happens. Forgiveness is a gift to ourselves and to the people around us.

Big hurts and betrayals cause the most difficulty and confusion. The true meaning of forgiveness is not forgetting. Forgiveness is not excusing offenses that would have caused us a life of more confusion and pain.

Forgiveness gives the forgiver peace of mind without destructive thinking due to the anger at the offense. We learn to love like God does, unconditionally. The importance of forgiveness is that it affects every area of our lives.

Forgiveness helps us move forward toward our future instead of trying to get revenge or to dwell in our pasts. Looking back can best be reserved to remember the goodness of God, not those mistakes we or others have made.

We become merciful with ourselves and other people we have encountered. We see others through the eyes of Jesus and his compassion and love instead of holding on to our hurts.

Learning how to forgive others means to surrender our will and control to God. We need to let the person off the hook and move on.

No matter how much hope and trust you had in that meaningful other person, the relationship will never be the same, nor will it continue. The feelings are gone, and both of you will ever feel the same way.

Acknowledging the feelings is not to rehash the situation, but to analyze and process the hurtful situation. God will help you work on overcoming your past dysfunction that ended in pain. Psalm 147:3.

Relationships and Boundaries

All relationships need boundaries. Following a lost relationship or conflict.

Your experiences were meant in love and neither meant to offend.

Forgiveness gives us boundaries because it unhooks us from the one who has been forgiven. If we do not take this healing step, we are continuing in a destructive relationship.

Becoming whole helps us resist the urge to keep going back so that we can move on and enjoy other healthy relationships.

Faithful forgiving is a personal battleground. We discover God's footprints in our souls. We all have God's image. God's grace is a spiritual gift that never fails. Grace reminds us of where we came from and to help us get unlocked when we are in a storm or conflict. God's grace is always with us to strengthen our faith and bring us peace. God loves the person who was hurt and the one who did the hurting. Two words Jesus spoke more than any others were forgiveness and mercy.

To be a Christian, we have to be different. Giving up a me-centered life where the human ego is supreme, faithfulness means to do the most difficult thing. Forgiveness is a choice. We choose to forgive. If we wait for someone to apologize to us, it might never occur. Feelings alone will not bring out our love needed for forgiveness. Forgiveness is difficult. For some it is impossible.

God gives the grace needed. We do the action. Another person walking with us is needed. The journey has the destination of forgiveness. Forgiveness frees us. Unforgiveness brings more pain and bitterness.

To forgive is just what the word itself says. To forgive is offering a gift before it has been earned or deserved. Forgiveness is not giving in, but to let go. If we do not forgive, we continue to be emotionally handcuffed to that person or persons who hurt us. Handcuffed people are not free. They never know the fruit of peace beyond all understanding. Forgiveness is like a boomerang: the gift we send out is what we are going to get back.

Sins against us does not define us. The love and grace of God defines us. Grace grows as e respond to sins committed against us. The beauty of life softens and unchains us as we forgive. Hebrews 12:15.

Forgiveness frees, sanctifies, and purifies. We journey on the road for healing and for experiencing joy that is unexplained in human terms. Psalm 51:12.

Numbers of studies confirm that forgiveness leads to better health. Forgiveness eses our depression, improves sleep. It reduces blood sugar, and it boosts the immune system. Forgive yourselves as you forgive others around you.

From genuine friendships to romantic partnerships, every human relationship is strengthened by forgiveness. Spouses need forgiveness. Without forgiveness, the traumas from childhood can go on into the adult years.

The Professional World Is Harsh

The professional world is harsh. We all eventually will be mistreated. We will be taken for granted by our bosses and even by colleagues. Forgiveness is essential to career success. Bosses are bossed by their bosses the very same way they mistreated you.

We choose forgiveness out of faithfulness to God. We recognize the command to forgive. I John 5:3, Psalm 119:32.

Faithfulness in prayer is confessing our sin, including the errors and mistakes we have been a part of that separates us from one another. Approaching God for forgiveness through grace is difficult. Praying is to come to consciousness of what has always been there. Prayer, silence, and solitude are moments of grace that awakens us to the possibilities in a corrective lens that removes our distortions. II Corinthians 4:16-17.

God's dream is to strengthen us in our personal uniqueness concerning our deadness. God calls us to be willing to pray in loving obedience by which we are transformed from death to eternal life.

Forgiveness is a condition in which the sin of the past is not altered. Inevitable consequences will not be changed. A fresh act is added to those in the past. Our broken relationship is restored. The blotting out of our sin and our restoration to wholeness comes with intimate praying. To be cleansed and accepting the cleansing we live as one forgiven and restored by grace.

Our outer life listens to our inner life. Jesus lives in our inner life. We sense that attraction that lifts our souls from the world. Love, joy, and grace are fruit that makes us free.

Without forgiveness, life will not change. Look at the nations hat harbor continuous hate. Look at the urban gangs in the United States and throughout the world whose goals are to destroy and kill other people. See our own troubled families.

If we continue to live in sin, deadness rules our lives. Romans 8:12-13. God touches the deeply ingrained structure of deadness. By grace, we come alive in the image of Christ. Continuing faithfulness through prayer is supported by others who share our brokenness. We need others to embrace us in love.

Forgiveness is difficult for those who have lived past the biblical "three score and ten." The fires lighted by sin are impossible to extinguish. For decades they wait for an apology that never comes. Hurts smolder. Their prayers are for the cool water of grace to flow until the fire ends.

Forgiveness sets us free. We must pray to become prepared with our own deep willingness to forgive those who have terribly harmed us. Praying has its own timing. We pray to be ready. We ask God to open our hearts as the snows of winter slowly melt. Forgiveness brings the joy of moving on. Moving on means to receive the gift of the Holy Spirit with the assurance of the love of God and forgiveness.

Forgiveness Opens the Windows of Our Souls

When we forgive, we are forgiven. Faithfulness in forgiving is throwing open the windows of our souls and allowing in fresh air and light. There are no restrictions or limits on forgiveness. Psalm 103:12, Jeremiah 31- 34, I John 1:9. To tell someone that they have sinned against you takes courage. The apostles asked Jesus to increase their faith. Jesus has given us the faith to forgive. The smallest grain of faith does amazing things. Uprooting a tree and throwing it into the sea without a heavy-duty machine is impossible to us.

The same is true in rebuking and forgiving someone over and over again. God wants us to be generous in our forgiveness. The disciples doubted their own ability to forgive. They thought it took some extra, extraordinary faith to forgive again and again.

As for forgiveness, we are to obey God. Even the apostles had to be reminded of their place in relation to God.

The baggage of keeping up appearances is relinquished. We let down our guard. Warm love comes in return. Repenting is not an option. Our sin has rippled out into the world community. Sin has grown in unexpected ways. Little sins are like a butterfly in Brazil flapping her wings and causing a tornado in Minnesota.

Imagine that. Identify a person whom you blame for mistreating or offending you. Imagine you are sitting down with that person or meeting them again on the street. Tell that person you forgive him or her and you feel empathy seeing that one's a whole person rather than as someone who has been defined by offensive behavior. What can you say? How do you feel? What does your facial expression look lie? What physical sensations do you notice?

Write a letter to the person but don't mail it. You can write a letter to anyone whom you have not forgiven, even if they are no longer in your life. Explain in the letter what they did that case much hurt and emotional pain, and what you wish you both had done instead. Finish the letter with a statement of forgiveness, such as: "I realize that you were doing the best you could at the time and the circumstances, and I forgive you."

In your journal you might reflect on what you have done. What rituals have you established to forgive? How would you like to be treated when you make mistakes? Have you managed to overcome resentment?

Jesus' quintessential parable on forgiveness is in Matthew 18:24-35. What does the king in the parable decides to do? A servant was "brought to him." The Greek indicates that this servant was dragged before the king. It would have been impossible to settle the debt. What would your reaction to the king's generosity? Based on your study of this biblical story, what is your own definition of forgiveness?

Be careful what you preach, write, and teach. A teacher affects eternity. You will know where your influence stops.

My son, I am the One who forgives you. Tell Me, what holds you back from past and present sins that continue to live in you. These sins still live in your heart. The heavenly Father wants to continue to set you free, even after we are saving you, the wrongs are fresh, will power to deceive and paralyze you.

Put those offenses away, rise up, and walk in faith with Me. Your journey on earth is among people who do not know right from wrong. Each generation lives in fogginess not faithfulness.

My Holy Presence is breathed throughout my creation and by grace re-created. May all remnants of your flesh be dissolved into ash by my holy fire.

I will continue to cleanse you from its dreadful grasp, a flow that is immersed in crimson power. You are still My Jim despite the storms you have endured.

I fully realize that life on earth is difficult. Joy is My gift that you might not always be feeling, but it is secure in your faithful soul. Life is so hard. Remember, I have overcome the world.

Intentionally look at Me. I am the One who carries you in the most stifling and frightful circumstances. Fear will never undo you. I have plans for you.

Do not turn your eyes inward. Circumstances delight and My job is etched on your face. I note that your eyes twinkle, and your smiles come without a thought.

Smiles show your joy and My joy even when your faith is shaken. Forgiveness works through our on-going willingness to give up certain claims against each other.

Our living theology depends on the depth of prayer, biblical understanding, mutual love, and vulnerable service. We are transformed into living images of God. Grace and conversion involves the whole inexhaustible meaning of merging into the reality of Christ. We are adopted in Christ. This means a deepening life of experienced relationships with God and discipleship in love and service to others.

Faith and forgiveness are inseparable. We are in the world, but not of the world. We have hoped to be faithful to a new vision of life, but as year passed, we were forced to admit we had not changed as we once thought.

Our transformation has been real, but it has become limited. God does not ask us to develop some goodness before coming to us. We must trust the integrity of our created lives and the faithfulness of God in the process of conversion.

Transmission of our souls happens secretly, quietly, and barely known consciously. It might takes years for us to become aware and to react to life on an eternal focus.

The process of faith is slow and difficult. The Holy Spirit moves at his or her own pace. Conversion leads us to simplify our lives. As we face our inner pain, we become willing not to pull away from full involvement in the pain and joy of life.

Out of our pain of early rejection, early isolation, early wounding from people close to us, we keep on with the patterns of separation in adult relationships.

The old must die before the new is born. There can be no union with God without transformation. God's transforming grace is celebrated with the emergence of new life. We become aware of how God and others love us. We become faithful to the new person we are now. We accept all of life including its brokenness. We can give up our fears. We find greater intimacy with our neighbors. We are no longer envious, because now we know who we are, and we celebrate that uniqueness.

We give up our false desires when we find abundance in God. Gradually, we find happiness and times of joy. Faithfulness will grow more and more each day.

We will be in the world, but not of it.

Chapter Three

DARKNESS AND FAITHFULNESS

Without faith, we are trapped in darkness. Weather in Nebraska is unpredictable. Activity outside can become intense. Heavy rainstorms and even tornadoes can show up with thunder crashing and lightning making gashes in the sky. One spring day a huge tree fell onto the roof. Dupree from other trees were seen throughout our lawn the next morning.

Within the faithful, there is darkness. We hide what is messy and dark. Parts of our life journey are so mind-bending that we don't tell most people. This driving force shows up in ordinary lives.

Some days are harder than others. Some mornings I am cheerful, even in the darkness. Other days I am overwhelmed. One day I am full of faith. During a difficult circumstance, I am empty and faithless. Psalm 77.

Some of us are better at facing the shadows. Our faith is shaken but the dark need not control us. Sometimes we must embrace the doubts within us. We cannot transform our dark thoughts into light thoughts. Sometimes we must just sit still. Darkness is part of you. Understand why it exists. It is part of the underworld.

Surrounded by uncertainty, we must reignite our faithfulness. Revival is our soul's cry before God in times of desperation and brokenness. This refreshing and reviving is unexpected by ordinary people.

Doubts make us feel unprepared for life's next challenge. We personalize difficult experiences. We doubt ourselves. Questioning is quite natural as it leads to concrete answers. Doubt expresses the "what if" and the "why" questions. Doubt in dark times focuses on the possibility that we were misled.

We do not have to feel guilty for our darkness. The thoughts that continue to surface hurt us because our culture teaches us that it is wrong to be down, depressed, or depleted. It is so sad that most people refuse to speak of it.

Vulnerability Grows in Darkness

Darkness makes us vulnerable. We must be careful and discerning about who we share our troubles with. Bushing off other people too quickly because they do not perceive faith as we do and might be rejecting help in dark times.

We are vulnerable if we live with people who enable our doubts by questioning and criticizing our decisions. What causes this experience to be worse, these same people will question our abilities, our capacity, and our talents.

I do not like to drive my car at night. My night vision gets dimer with each year. The Bible uses darkness as a metaphor for the fallen world. Our vision of eternity is clouded. Our spiritual eyesight becomes dim. We see through a glass darkly. God is omnipotent. God has power over darkness, over storms, gravity, the wind, fire and water. In times of darkness, God seems to be far away. During our own darkness, we are able to relate to those who have had similar experiences. Ecclesiastes reveals that there is nothing new under the sun. Not discovering another person who has been through the same storms in their lives would be impossible. We never have to walk alone. Psalm 23.

Faith is not sight. Faithfulness is not blindness. The uncertainties of faith are not the source of our despair. Faith in God purifies the notions that cloud our vision. To live by faith is an ongoing conversion. We need "night vision" to see the darkness. Our vision quests help us see with spiritual eyes.

God calls us out of darkness into divine light. I Peter 2:9. God gives the clear light of the world guiding us. Storms will continue to shake us until the end of time. Revelation tells of mountains and islands being removed. People are crying for rocks to fall on them.

God has purpose in dark and stormy days. It brings personal evaluation. After the times of waiting, God shakes us up to draw us back into a love relationship and an eternal fellowship. Everything we see and enjoy on earth is temporary. Our homes, bank accounts, and all that is in our control will soon not exist.

The Kingdom of God will not be shaken. The heavenly kingdom will be filled with love, joy, grace, peace, endurance, faithfulness, and self- control. Everything that is unshakeable will still be standing. Hebrews 12:28-29.

Divine Fire in the Unshakable Kingdom

As the children of God, divine fire will purify and transform us into something mature and perfect. The Holy Spirit gives us forward looking joy. Difficult and dark situations test our loyalty to God. God gives us the Spirit in order for us to become more like Jesus.

Remembering and writing about our own life stories are remarkable evidence of the times God has helped me. I now have shoeboxes full of pretty rocks with the places where I picked them up during my journeys. They are my stones of remembrance. An early one recounts my conversion as an eight-year-old. Another was found on the front lawn of Tennessee High School in Bristol, where I preached my first sermon at age 12. Looking through my rock collection, I recall unmistakable encounters. I remember where I was and what was happening when I sensed God speaking to me.

Looking at these rocks buoys my faith. I gain courage for trust in the present time. I Kings 17, we read the story of Zarephath's flour and oil. She never knew if she would have enough for the next day. She had no resources of her own. Her story shows us how God provides for us.

Nobody wants to live with scarcity. We feel utterly vulnerable. We desire to have a full oil flask and an overflowing floor jar. Trusting God in the darkness is frightening.

Times of darkness bring an uneasy feeling such as when losing a book manuscript that had been worked on for several months, getting news that you lost a job, a divorce or death, In those dark times, we lose wholeness. We feel rejected. Thankfully, most days are normal. Nothing negative happens. Life is smooth sailing much of the time.

The faith that was once comfortable is now too shaky to support us. Without faith, we are like non-swimmers in an ocean without water wings to keep us floating in the water. Without faith, we are trapped in darkness. Dark times teach us to respect the simple routine of getting up, going to work, and spending a quiet evening at home. Shaken faith periods are temporary. God shows up in our darkest times.

We are consumed with our own comfort. God is consumed with our eternal joy. Our places of famine and desolation have become the places where we see God clearly.

Darkness and Faith Dynamics

Our times of storms and darkness help us understand the dynamics of faith. When the ground beneath us rocks and shifts, we wonder. Life is never the same after a loss or tragedy. The same dynamics are at work after a great joy. Matthew 5:45.

God will give us the grace to accept life's crosses and joys. God's mysterious ways are not meant to hurt us. Life is an endless adventure moved by forces beyond our control. More things are going on than we perceive with our limitations. I have encountered countless people who refused to be destroyed by a trauma that plunged them into darkness. They chose life. If people could understand how to find the light that gets us out of darkness, their shaken faith would become strong faith. Life on earth is filled with hardships, tragedies, defeats, and losses. This is our human destiny. Faithfulness is enduring what we must and changing what we can.

That is a definition of faithfulness. It is not to make us always feel good. Faithing is done in the darkness and in the lightness. God continues to use us and to transform us into the image of the faithful.

The best book on faith and faithfulness was edited by Brain Kolodiejchuk. The title is *Mother Teresa, Come Be My Light: The Private Writings of the Saint of Calcutta.* This more than 400 pages is filled with commentary in the darkness of the faith journey. Most of the material has never been published until this one. Mother Teresa was well aware of the uncommon circumstances of her calling and how she experienced it. Reading it will challenge everything we have thought about faithful saints.

In her annual retreats, she would review her life and renew her commitment to strive after faithfulness. Her faith was much stronger than my own faith as I serve Jesus as minister of joy to the world. The editor of her works gave us insight into her ministry. He wrote, "To commit herself to becoming an apostle of joy, when humanly speaking, she might have felt in the brink of despair, was heroic indeed. She could do so because her joy was rooted in the certitude of the ultimate goodness of God's loving plan for her. And though her faith in this truth did not touch her soul with consolation, she ventured to meet the challenge of life with a smile." (Brian Kolodiejchuk, editor, p. 171)

Teresa wanted us to remember that love begins at home. In many of her letters and writings, she insisted that only by first loving those closest would be her religious family become builders of peace that she wanted us all to be. She distributed a little card as her business card. One of her well-known sayings was printed on it. The words on it were: "The fruit of silence is prayer. The fruit of prayer is faith. The fruit of faith is love. The fruit of love is service. The fruit of service is peace." (Brian Kolodiejchuk, pp. 314-315)

God Never Stops Working

God never stops working in our dark days. These days refine us. You can love someone in deep despair without falling into their darkness. Finding our way through the darkness is part of the faith journey.

Faith is essential when God's promises contradict what we are seeing. Faith is an opponent of fear. Faith protects us from the consequences of fear. Faith erodes fear. Ephesians 6:13-17. Faithfulness means that we need not fear worldly troubles. The will of God is always to our benefit. We do not only endure, but we fully live by faith.

For faith to become strong, it must go through darkness. We go through a lot of experiences, storms, and trials. Shallow faith collapses under difficulties. In dark times, God wants us to believe, to be stripped of that which is not faith. God does not accept the situation in which we base our faith on actions, feelings, or experiences. Relying on our natural understanding, our clearness of reasoning will vanish. We go through a dark painful cleansing to gain strong faith.

When we are placed in difficult situations, we are provoked into doing acts of faith. During the darkness, we realize our powerlessness. We will deepen our yearning for God. Faith looks for God to come. The intensity of looking for God to come shows our faith in God. Faith is expressed in our need for God. Our growth in faith will be indicated by our continuous looking and spiritual hungering.

When God wants us to reach the depths of faith, difficult trials will face us. God takes away our human supports. Becoming uprooted without securities from humans, causes us to look for redemption from God alone.

Pouring my heart out to God comforts me. I experience joy only after I have acknowledged my pain. This was the case for Jeremiah 15:18; for Job 7:11, 14-16; Habakkuk 1:2; and David in Psalm 13:1-2.

Abraham is the father of our faith. God uprooted Abraham. Genesis 12:1. Abraham rooted in his native Haran, not far from Ur. He became increasingly reliant on God. Abraham asked God what was expected. Abraham's faith and entrustment to God was born from being uprooted and from his uncertainty. Faith is never easy for any of us.

God Places Us in Difficult Situations

The more the promises of God appear to be unlikely, but God does miracles. God desired to raise Abraham's trust to the peak. During darkness he trusted God. Our most difficult situations are of particular advantage because they demand crucial decisions.

God sometimes places us in difficult situations. We cannot cope with it. We will look for God to come. It is impossible for us to remain in stagnation. We might not answer God's desire. We will tend to retreat in faith. Or, like Abraham, we will entrust ourselves to grace and faith.

Darkness is a stage on the way toward God. Every difficult situation is a time of dryness. We will look into our inner selves and discover who we are. We will also discover which is most important.

Writing in my journals, I express my deepest feelings to God. I write of my disappointments mixed with my doubt and anger. I tell my Love that I don't feel loved. Then I hear the Supreme Being whisper that my forgiving Father has loved me with eternal love.

Darkness can be experienced by an entire nation. God places us in difficult situations through internal and external experiences. The darkness is a grace. God who loves us is present in the dark times. Darkness reveals what is hidden. Layers of human passions and evil bring terrifying truth about us.

Times of Darkness Incites the Overcoming of Lukewarmness

The gift of darkness helps us overcome lukewarmness. It forces us to make choices. As long as we remain lukewarm and things go well for us without problems, our situations in the light of faith are tragic.

The ultimate reason for darkness is revealed in the book of Revelation chapter three: 15-16. Lukewarmness in a person is unacceptable. It is repulsive to God. The darkness will transform us as a place where faith is born. Faithfulness deepens to the extent of denudation. God will fill us with Presence to the extent that we will delude ourselves and follow the call of God and love.

God reminds us that the more of this mutual, mysterious relationship deepens, the greater our need for denudation. That is the way of the calling of God that a person who loves God will go beyond human capacities. God expects a lukewarm person of little faith, to become zealous in the faith and in self-surrender.

Faith does not remove darkness. Faith requires the dark times. The events of being stripped of supports can bring joy for one who loves God. Darkness brings an opportunity to profess our love for God with faithfulness. God responds to sin and human weakness with love. Experiencing darkness helps us to discover our need for God and to realize that we are completely dependent.

Time is priceless because it is the presence of God. The essence of Christian faith is continuing to say to God: "Thy will be done." Darkness is not meant to be our dwelling place. It is a pathway, a highway on which we come to know the merciful love of God.

God will give us rest in the dark times just like we sleep in the night hours. Psalm 42:5, 43:5. We will remember the deeds of the Lord. God's deeds are done for divine glory.

Peace in the Darkness

God will give us a joyful peace in the darkness. That joy is unexplainable. Will we choose to set our eyes on our Redeemer? Psalm 73:25-28. A faithful life does not get a lot of accolades. Faithful people are often overlooked. Faithing is not glamorous. It requires moving in the direction down a long and windy road. The desired destination is just ahead.

The faith of faithfulness is believing in the unseen. Our life of perceived prominence is no more significant that a life of faithfulness. Perhaps our faithfulness in the long run will bring us a larger influence. Prominence may get in the way of faithfulness. We overcome doubt and darkness through faith in God, who is bigger than our perceived problems. We see God's perspective. Only then, can we become conquerors. Romans 8:37.

God has declared that if we are faithful in little things that we will be given more and greater things. If not, faith alone is what makes us work in ways true to the plan of God. This work and focus sometimes feels like we take three steps forward and two steps backward. We feel that we are losing life.

Jesus declares that one day the faithful will hear him say, "Well done, good and faithful servant. You have been faithful over little things; I will set you over much." Matthew 25:23. These words are heavenly words. Heaven's atmosphere is pure joy. Joy will be the air we breathe. Our Lord is inexhaustible. The Joy of the Lord is inexhaustible. A season of doubt is an opportunity to grow in our spiritual understanding.

The Holy Spirit is there to empower, to direct, and to guide us as we become "more than conquerors." Doubt is a way to truth and life. Doubts are like messengers from God. We cannot avoid it. Honest believers struggle about the existence of God, about Jesus' uniqueness, and where we will go when we die.

Doubts are normal. They are potentially formative. Doubting brings a deadening, anger with God, and thinking we have been misled. Thinking this way brings on more apathy, paralysis, and spiritual limping along.

C.S. Lewis describes faith as the art of holding on to things you once thought reasonable. (C.S. Lewis *Mere Christianity*, pp. 121-122) If faith is unattended, there is a slowdown in life satisfaction, self-esteem, and positivity. Doubt debilitates as it saps the pep out of our step, locking our feet in cement.

Eventually, we see the world as meaningless. This is the root of mistrust. It is a deep crisis in faith. God loves us. Doubt is common and natural. We need not feel guilty or ashamed for questioning.

Doubt is not a sin. However, it has led some to the temptation to sin. Nobody is immune to doubting. Simply telling others, or us, to just stop doubting is no solution. Doubt is the temptation to disbelieve what God has said.

When Jesus took on the human condition, he became like us in every respect, except without sin. Hebrews 2:17-18. We must stick with our profession even when we are unsure. Jesus becomes our high priest. We receive mercy and grace, as Jesus fulfills the role of the high priest. Hebrews 4:14-16.

Jesus enables us to reignite our hope. Experiencing God's love, joy, and grace in times of disappointment and doubt, brings an unexpected revival. Doubt can be a doorway to intimacy with God. Faith is intermeshed with fear. This surprising revival brings us to God who does the impossible. God always does the best for us. Ezekiel 11:19-20, 20:42.

We never have to lose heart. We realize the call of God. We reawaken our purpose when we experience revival in our souls.

Darkness helps us understand the light. Light allows us to know what darkness is. We can continue to love ourselves in dark times. We can be comfortable. We can be healed and liberated.

Darkness is a metaphor for the fallen world where we live. Our vision of eternity is clouded. Our spiritual eyesight becomes dim. Darkness causes us to be vulnerable.

God allows darkness so that the divine can work with us and to shape our faith. Grace is multiplied through our trials. Like refined gold, God brings us through the fire. Having our faith shaken is not weakness, but a characteristic of our humanity. We are not to condemn ourselves.

God will never forsake us. Singing "Great Is Thy Faithfulness," gives me assurance. Singing the words brings confidence into my own personal vision quest.

Heaven will never be shaken. The heavenly kingdom is based on love, peace, and faithfulness. The unshakeable will still be standing. Hebrews 12:28-29.

When a church family gathers, we often sing, "Heaven came down, and glory filled our souls."

My joyful and surrendered minister, I was there with you in your dark times. It is important for you to stay open to My Wisdom with your faith even in the darkness. Darkness cannot not drive out darkness, only My Light can do that. People have a deep fear of darkness. Darkness is like a window to the unknown. Known to Me always, but not to you.

I will show up in your life in My own ways in the hour you don't expect Me. In this time of uncertainty, you may doubt, but don't stop believing. I will tell you now that the outcome on the other side is ultimately certain and sure. It is firm, secure, and good.

Put aside the deeds of darkness and put on the armor of My light. Arise in the stillness in the early morning hours as your life continues to be filled with shadows. You were sleeping peacefully, resting in a slumber. You will hear the sound of My voice that speaks in the darkness. You may hear the soft sound of a bird before dawn breaks.

In these loving moments, you will be quiet and hold calmingly ethereal peace. The high points of our relationship with me are connected to the low points in our dark circumstances. The ways of God are not what you expect. Only in desperation do we hear My call.

Disappointment, lost dreams, sorrow, and suffering are invitations from Me. Trials in the darkness, the rain, the storms, the hardest nights are mercies in disguise.

Any misfortune that places you in the darkness will cause you to feel uneasy. It is natural for any human being to be afraid of the dark. It is the darkest just before dawn. Helen Keller braved a lot of darkness. She once said, "Walking with a friend at night is better than walking alone in the light."

Martyn Lloyd-Jones sermons and books put darkness in perspective. Remember God loves you as the Father loves Jesus. Remember, I love you. Nothing separates you from My love. I have sympathy for you in your weakness. I understand your suffering. I weep with you in your pain, I call you by your name. I constantly intercede and discern your fears.

I guide your circumstances during dark times. Life depends on your focus. My glory is proven when you demonstrate that your soul is satisfied in Me alone. (D. Martyn Lloyd-Jones, *Spiritual Depression: Its Causes and Cures*, pp. 20-22)

I will bring you My Light into your times of darkness. Live your life in the time you are living here on earth. Wait for My coming in glory. I shall spiritually heal you.

I will give you grace-filled signs. I have come to you to fulfill all your hopes and dreams. I shall offer you visions of joy and peace.

My Jim, believe Me when I tell you that I am with you in dark times. I will give your spiritual eyes clearing sight. I know that you are amazed when earthly securities dissolve.

I heard the sound of a lark on one of your dark days. In the dark, I know you heard the gentle sound of that lark.

Darkness sits inside of you. You can do nothing about it by yourself. Look beyond your weaknesses and failed attempts. Reach for a reality that makes sense of all of life. I am the source of that reality.

I give your life a purpose. My grace and love give you saving faith. I am the source of your energy needed to stop nursing your ills, giving in to despair, flaunting your achievements, and battering your soul for mere trinkets.

Faith grows in the dark. Faith is in your not knowing, but fully trusting me. If you were always certain of the outcome, it would not be faithful. The power of darkness is like a powerful magnet. Don't lose your soul to the allure of darkness.

Chapter Four

STORMS AND FAITHFULNESS

Snowstorms are a way of life in Nebraska. I have lived in Nebraska for 25 years. I have risked my life to preach as I drove through snowy roads. In another book, I wrote about the big blinding storm on my way home from Weeping Water in 2015. A storm watch was predicting a storm later that Sunday. I had made my way to church easily, but on my way home, blinding snow made visibility zero. The snow started as I walked out the door. Several inches accumulated quickly. It was freezing cold.

Nobody dared stop. The snow gripped beneath the tires. I forged ahead trying to follow the line of cars ahead of me. I forged ahead. I placed my faith in God's faithfulness as I prayed.

I had to handle my fear. I knew that I faced the possibility of a car crash that would have killed me. Although this was an unpredictable snowstorm, the same tactics and faithing would apply in other storms of life. Isaiah 43:2.

The snowstorms and Icey roads that I traveled all had an eventual ending. Storms vary by duration, type, and magnitude. Christ offers us a safe harbor of peace in the middle of a storm. Within our communities Christ tries to calm the sea of division. In our blindness to the values of other people, we celebrate our own stories and ignore the stories of other people's journeys. In the midst of life's storms, God is there. In the times of dark and terror, God is there.

For the winter of 2022-2023, Nebraska had a record snow and a minus 70-degree wind chill factor. Much of the whole United States had record low temperatures. Many people died from the cold frigid air, including hundreds of the homeless.

Remember Mordecai faced a possible death in his life storm. Esther was part of divine intervention. The apostle Paul wrote about his thorn in the flesh. We all have them. Storms will always part of our life journey. Storms come in a variety of ways besides the weather and unexpected turns of nature.

On a cold dark night in a German prisoner camp, the POW commandant ordered everybody to their barracks where they had to endure beatings. They felt so discouraged.

One of the prisoners began to pray the Lord's Prayer out loud. Those nearby joined in. The praying was overheard throughout the camp, and they joined the others in a growing chorus.

Hundreds of voices raised together as the said, "For thine is the kingdom, and the power and the glory, forever and ever. Amen."

The camp then was silent.

Hebrews 12:28 tells us the kingdom cannot be shaken. Believing in a faith that cannot be shaken is difficult when you or someone you love is shaking like a leaf.

The Dutch painter Ludolf Backhuysen painted a storm at sea. Two-thirds of his painting is covered in swirling gray clouds. I often use my oil paintings of waves as I did for the cover of my book on peace.

As I read Ecclesiastes, I see dark hues, and expressions on "vanity of vanities." I interpret it as a message of joy in a world of storm-tossed darkness.
I do not read it as a book of pessimism. Joy is repeated in the midst of frustrations and shaken faith. Ecclesiastes 2:24-26, 3:12-15, 5:18-20, 8:15-20, 9:7-10, 11:8-12:7.

God gifts the gift of joy to the faithful despite the poverty of brokenness and shaking faith. The book does not teach that life is meaningless. Life is beautiful. Ecclesiastes is honest concerning our lives' vanities. We must grieve concerning vain things. Ecclesiastes 2:24-26.

The thesis is summarized in the book's conclusion in 12:13-14. These are the final words, "the end of the matter."

There is no security in our vain world except through faith in God. God will one day make everything right. We can choose to cling to joy despite the fact that everything—our works, our accumulations, our legacies—are gone when we die. Only eternal things will last forever. We cling to joy when everything appears out of control.

Faithful people do not depend on quick fixes. Peace comes because of our faith and faithfulness. At the end of this part of holy scripture, we are told to "fear God" and to keep the commandments of God. As we interpret the Hebrew, this means "to worship God." Worship re-centers us in the glory of God.

Confidence in the glory and grace of God offers the basis for joy in the darkness we experience. The joy of God is our strength. Even in the midst of vanity and pain and suffering. We are still to rejoice in "all" the years of our lives.

Finding God in Pain and Illness

Recently I was stooping over with painful arthritis in my spine. I had poor posture. I walked as one living in a nursing home. Luke 13 has the story of the stooped women that Jesus encountered. She had endured sharp pain for nearly 20 long years. She was bent over low, looking down at her feet. She was regarded by her community as damaged goods. Everyone looks away, ignoring her. Jesus notices her. Wen Jesus saw her, he called out to her, Woman, you are free from your sickness." Jesus walked over to her. He placed his hands on her shoulders. Up and down her spine, he squeezed life and love into her trembling body. He straighten up tall and praised God.

Hope in a Shaky World

What gives us hope in an unshakable kingdom? Is there hope in a shaky world?

Living with sickness or pain is so difficult. Where is God in all of this? People become embittered and turn away from faith. They cannot see pain and suffering as a spiritual opportunity. God does not initiate any new consciousness.

The glory of life can't be realized until there is no more death, no more sickness, no more suffering. That is God's goal despite the storms, finding new ways to enjoy life, accepting disability and the knowledge that the things we love to do are now lost forever.

Jesus gathers us around him. Those who have become stooped by oppression and shame are freed to stand to their full height as the sons and daughters of God.

Jesus cares about the storms we face. He brings us through them. Mother Teresa wrote, "Since then I have kept this promise—and when sometimes darkness is very dark—and I am on the verge of saying no to God, the thought of that promise pulls me up." (Brian Kolodiejchuk, *Mother Teresa: Come Be My Light: The Private Writings of the Saint of Calcutta*, p. 187)

During our trials of faith, we sense a crisis. Faith in the face of difficulties often begins to collapse. Our feelings and our emotions are all mixed up. We cannot count on ourselves. Faith relies on the love and grace of God. If that inner tension remains to push us into panic in the face of fears and threats, our will and our thoughts are overcome in the haste. We have no peace.

Faith keeps us believing in love. Christs needs nothing for himself. Love is bound up with eternal life. Loved ones await for us in heaven.

Faithing is often simple and joyful. At times it can become a struggle, a fight, a decision that isn't spontaneous. Faith demands courage. Every person who lives on earth has lived through difficult days with suffering and deep darkness. These situations are normal in the spiritual life. Times of trial are needed. Our illusions fall away. Our faith grows with no emotional foundation. God alone sustains our faith. Faith uses scripture, which has grace, a particular authority that reforms our faith. Luke 12:7. Trails end by the beginning of a new day of joy.

Unshaken Faith Comes in Grace

God aims toward an unshaken faith within us. Trials become graces. Live as if it is our last day on earth. It could well be.

Christ is fully aware of our struggles. He has promised he will never leave us nor forsake us. Deuteronomy 31:6. We will realize we could drown in the waves of our storm. These storms will eventually make us stronger.

Jesus is always near to us as we cry out to him. He never disappoints us. Dark storms leave us in shock. Controlled and comfortable life is shattered. Without faith, we are like non-swimmers in the oceans without water wings. Without faith, darkness traps us.
Faith is deepened when we experience the storms of life. The storm on the sea described in Scripture is symbolic for our life situations. During difficult trials of faith, we think Jesus has abandoned us. Storms of worry about the future, storms of temptations, storms about health, storms concerning work, storms involving discord in marriage.

The faces of the apostles were contorted in fear. Jesus' peaceful face was relaxed as he was sleeping. Every storm can be a purpose. God is passing by

71

which brings grace. Jesus told them that they lacked adequate faith. This caused fear and panic. With his gesture of sleeping, he was trying to show them that he wanted to say, "I am with you, be calm, for nothing can happen to the boat that I am in." Our faith and belief in the fact that he is present and close to us. He makes us peaceful and calm despite our emotional state. Storms are tests of faith. The disciples were Jews and had read the psalms which told of how God calms the seas. Psalm 107. They had been taught that whatever threatened them, God would be there for them.

We can imagine a deep hush as the disciples looked at Jesus. Each was caught up in their own thoughts. They were still breathing heavily. I can imagine their hearts still pounding. They were uncertain who Jesus was. They were getting acquainted with Jesus and this storm happened in his early ministry.

I wonder what was more terrifying, seeing what Jesus could do or that they were in the presence of the Messiah. They concluded that God was in the midst of the storms of life.

We are fearful about our future. Some fears are outside of us. Often, they reside within us. We are afraid of the unknown. Earthly fears are endless. These include being fearful concerning or health or income security or our safety or the future of our church.

We must prepare for the next storm that will come. Faithfulness does not mean avoiding difficulties. Facing storm clouds does not mean God doesn't care.

"Peace be still." When storm clouds gather, when life circumstances overwhelm, remember God is with us in the boat. "Peace be still" is a praise to travel with us and to remind us of God's abiding care.

God is love. Steadfast love endures forever. When there is rough water ahead, turn to God.

When storms come into our lives, external or internal, look into the face of Jesus. Storms do not always strengthen faith. If we reject the stripping of ourselves, then we retreat from entrusting self to God. Faith in the face of difficulties starts to collapse. Haste, stress, and anxiety as symptoms of little faith or lack of faith.

Hurricane Ian devastated Central Florida. Floods and tornados demand that we find a safe place. It is human fearful, frightened, and faithless in a deadly situation. When storms come, seek to be at peace as Jesus was calm. Jesus knew a weather pattern was forming, churning into a dangerous storm.

In one moment, everything is peaceful. In the next moment we find ourselves surrounded by a storm. In every storm we face in life, no matter the seemingly insurmountable the problem is, God provides a way of escape. I Corinthians 10:13.

Whenever, we take difficult situations into our own hands, we are simply counting on yourself. We are pushing Jesus aside, and saying, "I cannot count on you." Difficult graces of the trials of faith involve suffering that is accepted with the closeness of Christ.

Living in the Present Moment

Live in the present moment. Live as if this was our last day on earth. Tomorrow is not certain. Yesterday does not belong to us. Do not look back. Luke 9:62.

Trials of faith strengthen self-entrusting to Jesus. "Peace be with you," "shalom." John 14:27. The world can give us human peace. When there is no human peace left, fear appears. We depend on human moods and whims. During our storms, God is not in heaven wringing hands and wondering what will happen to you. God is not weak. Even Jesus' disciples had to learn to trust Jesus by the doubt creating circumstances they faced.

Things happen that shake our faith. Situations arise suddenly like a storm. Shaking us up. Spinning us around. Overwhelming our emotions. Faith is not shaken in days of calm. When faith is shaken, we are confused. We can hold onto our faith amid being shaken. Trust is being put on trial. When our faith becomes unsteady, there are things we can hold onto. Stick with what you know. In my prayer journals I can see all my answered prayers. I write my testimony day after day and year after year.

When my faith is shaken from my soul, I experience fear, anger, guilt, anxiety, and everything in between. This world wears on me. Other people wear on me. My faith remains strong. Faith is my bedrock.

President Abraham Lincoln said, "I have been driven many times to my knees by the overwhelming conviction that I had nowhere else to go."

I have depended on airlines to fulfill my ministry to the world. In several of my trips, violent thunderstorms have leveled off in the distance at cruising altitude. As my flight drew closer to the thunderstorm, passengers became nervous and fearful about the storm. Isaiah 41:10.

Storms of life knock the wind out of us. Reach out. There are people and resources that are readily available. Having faith shaken is not a sign of weakness. We are all ordinary humans.

I the midst of our personal storms, God has a firm grip on us. When we need the peace of God in our lives, deliverance from storms of adversity, read Jeremiah 29:12-14. We can always learn faithfully with every storm. Philippians 4:11. God clearly wants us to learn how to live blessed, full of joy in each situation. God is incredibly faithful. We can sing "Great Is Thy Faithfulness."

Pain in my spine and back has kept my body on edge. I have been drained emotionally. My physical activity gets less and less. I have in the last few years walked with my back crooked over to one side like most people living in nursing homes. I have sought help from many physicians, but none could determine the cause of my pain in my muscles and joints. Physical therapy did not help me. I knew that God could heal, but like the apostle Paul I suffered a thorn in my flesh. My pain that sometimes felt like pieces of glass jarring my bones was being allowed by God for a purpose.

I prayed moment by moment for healing. My faith was tested as I prayed again and again for relief. My shoulders and spine reached their pain limit. One Sunday morning after I had preached in the chapel of an assisted living care center, I walked to my car and felt little pain. My spine became God's spine. My weakness was strengthened by the will of God.

My pain and suffering was infused by the joy of God. My back pain was a mountain I could not overcome in my life. Mark 16:17-18.

Jesus told us that we will do even greater works then he did on earth. John 14:26. By the power of the Holy Spirit, we are able to lead people to an encounter with Christ. Seeing people grow in faith to move past their mountains of doubt to experience salvation is the greatest work of all.

I have seen and felt mountains move. Faithfulness takes a leap into the will of God and rests in the knowledge of grace. My prayer has always been that somehow, I could reach out to the world concerning the joy of faithfulness.

I had published books with Broadman Press, the publishing arm of the

Southern Baptists and Abingdon Press of the United Methodists. Today I know God provided a way for me beyond my imagination. David Tullock had been searching how to reach people for Christ was encouraged by my life friend and mentor John Killinger to try Christian publishing. David is a Carson-Newman University and Southern Baptist Theological Seminary graduate. He called his publishing company Parson's Porch. It has grown rapidly. My books have miraculously reached the world. Google "Books by James McReynolds" and you can see what God has done through the faith and faithfulness demonstrated.

The peace of Christ flows from his presence. It is a gift. Ephesians 2:14. Accepting peace from Christ through faith is accepting Jesus. It is opening our souls totally to God. Peace is the fruit of spiritual life, the fruit of faith, deepened by trials. If someone or somethings stands between you and God, then you can't have faith or peace. This faith and peace involve permanent joy. It is fully believing in love. We do not know what is good for us. We are not able to love ourselves. To believe and love Jesus is to love what he wants, to love his will. Loving the will of Christ is confirmed by our choices during trials of faith that brings peace, love, and joy.

The artist Vincent Van Gogh said, "For those who believe in Christ, there is no sorrow that is not mixed with hope. There is only a constant being born again, a constantly going from darkness to light." (Anthony Wainwright, *Moment of Truth*, p. 123)

Strength Coming from Storms of Life

When people experience a disaster, many turn to God. Tornadoes, hurricanes, volcanic eruptions or floods interlace with finding the grace of God. Most attribute the absence of death and destruction to the intervention of God. Laid low in spirit, the storms can actually be the way we grow stronger on the inside as the fruit of faithfulness arrives.

The storms of life come disguised in many shapes that are found in differing situations. These storms look like fires, floods, endemics, divorce counts, hospital emergency rooms, fires, hospices, hijacked airplanes, revolutions, nuclear power plants, embassies with hostages, and homes where mental illness and drug abuse prevail.

These storms stir us to turn to God, adjust to the darkness, and some despair. They all acknowledge the limitations of the human condition and God's unlimited power. God's powerful and loving hand is eternally working, touching us with love, giving us grace for transformational change.

They never worry about being smart, logical, or powerful. They are entrenched in the ending of existence. They cry out for the unending existence in the Supreme Being.

Faith is tested in these dark times. We must consider the mystery or be stuck with our pain and suffering, the seeds for awakening. Job 38-39. God passionately loves us and our world. Great is God's faithfulness. God invites Job into a warm and personal encounter. Life is not solely about us. Faith means to be overwhelmed by the reality of God. God suffers our pain with us. When hard times come and the wintry winds of adversity
blow, joy will be ours as we let go and release. We see it in faith, as a testing of our hope and patience. We must not give up. We cannot lose heart.

Storms of Life, Souls Letting Go

Storms of life are wrapped in spiritual contemplation. We can take charge within our free will. Taking charge means to surrender the dead leaves. We take on God's grace gifts of love that will come our way. The appear to be hidden, concealed, and invisible. In time, our lives open up and our light shines.

Looking back on our lives and our faithing, we realize that the process is not finished. We struggle with it. It is confusing. It defines us. It is our most receptive path for endurance, patience, and resilience made possible by grace.

The trees in the Elmwood Park in front of our home are gorgeously maroon, yellow, orange, and a combination of color as they let go and fall to the ground. Our souls let go in a similar way.

During the days that our family experienced my wife's breast cancer surgery, we were sent words of hope in an email that encourage all of us.

"Fall in love with what's hard. It is what will hold you in the future. Fall in love with yourself as you go through the hard things. The transformation that comes from really being fully in the hard moments, times, and seasons are the graces, beauty, strength, and wisdom that will unshakably hold you in the future. These moments are holy, made just for you, making you. Your life is your medicine, even the hard parts."

Our Heavenly Father is waiting to shield us from the storms. Our Lord is ever ready to empower and enlighten us to accomplish our destiny. Never be discouraged during difficult times.

Singing Brings Joy to the Journey

We cannot know what our future holds, but we know our hope in Christ is secure. Singing songs is a powerful tool to reinforce the truth during our difficult times.

People forget quotes from our sermons, but they might know every word of songs of faith. "It Is Well With My Soul" has lyrics, "When peace like a river, attended my way, when sorrows like the sea billows roll; whatever my lot, Thou has taught me to say, 'It is well with my soul."

"Great Is Thy Faithfulness" is another. "Great is thy faithfulness. Great is thy faithfulness, morning by morning new mercies I see. And all I have needed thy hand hath provided, great is thy faithfulness Lord unto me."

Another worship song, "Lord From Sorrows Deep I Call." The lyrics are: "Storms within my troubled soul questions without answers on my faith these billows roll. God, be now my shelter. Why are you casting down my soul? Hope in Him that saves you when the fires have all grown cold cause this heart to praise you."

These moving songs are filled with words from the Holy Scripture. Another one is "I Will Wait for You" from Psalm 130. "Out of the depths I cry for you. In darkest places I will call. Incline your ear to me anew. And hear my cry for mercy, Lord."

"Lord, I Need You" is helpful in our troubled storms. "Lord, I come, I confess. Bowing here I find my rest. Without You I fall apart. You're the one that guides my heart."

A song of assurance in the days of darkness is "He Will Hold Me Fast." I heard it sung during a retreat at Conception Abbey near Maryville, Missouri. "When I fear my faith will fail, Christ will hold me fast When the tempter would prevail, he will hold me fast. I could never keep my hold trough life's fearful path, for my love is often cold. He must hold me fast."

Perhaps my readers have other music with everything inside that watches the darkness flee in the middle of the mysteries of our days of living in the world.

Great is thy faithfulness to me.

I know that there is hope for our shattered hearts. I write as one who experienced suffering with my close family and friends. I could never go through these trying times to reveal how we can become more like Christ.

The difficult storms have taught me grace and gratitude. It is easy to be thankful when things in life are going well. We can see God at work all around us even when circumstances are hard.

The strength of the joy of our Lord comes with financial, housing, relationships, and all illness including cancer and heart problems. We wonder when joy will surprise us again. My faith taught me that joy would be in my future. As I processed about my grief and suffering, God brought moments of joy in my mourning. These storms of life demonstrated that joy comes not when everything has been resolved.

In my book on peace that passes understanding, I attempt to see what real peace is. Peace is much more than just being calm. Peace is in the presence of God, not in the absence of difficulty.

This world tells us we need perfect beauty, health, wealth, bigger and newer things. None of that matters when death is near. We become crystal clear concerning our faith and our values. Philippians 3:8.

Real strength results from storms. We handle the mild annoyances and daily problems. Storms bring us to the end of our selves. We become completely dependent on God. God gives us the wisdom to replace our fears with faith. Strength comes to battle our storms. II Corinthians 12:9.

Faithfulness results from our storms. It appears easy to quote the promises of God when life is good. Faith proves those promises. We know faith during storms that we never see on sunny days. Faith and faithfulness become deeply personal. Psalm 25:10.

We experience firsthand how God meets our needs and cares for us. Miracles happen that we could never imagine.

Storms can teach us about the real home of the faithful. Difficulties teach us that this world is not our home. Storms are reminders that this time living on earth is temporary.

We let go of things that do not really matter in the long run, or in the short run. The storms help us turn our focus from building our own kingdom to building the kingdom of God.

As devastating as storms can be, the Bible tells us that our light and momentary troubles are accomplishing and achieving for us an eternal joy that far outweighs them all." II Corinthians 4:17.

There is no such person as one who is immune from the storms of living in the kingdom of man. When they do hit, God has assured us that difficulties will come.

Just like in times of tornados, hurricanes, financial depressions, fatal accidents, and deadly illnesses, we must be prepared.

We must trust our eternal life to God to ensure our souls will ultimately be spared. We strengthen our faith through intimate times for prayer, reading the Holy Scripture for assurance. Faithful obedience despite the temptations to disobey. We can join with other faithful believers to gather as a body and help weather the storms together. It's impossible to do it on your own.

Several years ago, I preached a six-point sermon at the First Christian Church in Weeping Water, Nebraska.

I. Faith calms us in the middle of a storm.
II. Faith does not always take us out of the problem.
III. Faith takes us through the problem.
IV. Faith does always take away the pain.
V. Faith gives us the ability to handle the pain.
VI. Faith does not take us out of the storm.

Our church vision was to create an atmosphere where joy and miracles happen. People in pain were drawn to the joy which only Jesus and his faithful followers can give. Storms will always be a part of our life journey. At one point in our ministry, we prayed in groups of three for 100 days.

Jim, I can walk on water during storms. I realize that water is a scary place. Humans can drown in it. Just ask Peter when you see him in heaven. I remember watching you enjoy the South Holston Lake, and the many creeks you enjoyed.

Water is a place for storms and hurricanes like Hurricane Ian. My world contains destructive storms like typhoons and tsunamis, and floods. Terrible winds sweep people out of the safety of our boat.

I make storms cease. These watery storms symbolize various storms including fires, accidents, and the things that come in our darkness. I have heard you write, crying in rage, doing what you don't want to do.

I will give you faith to overcome the storms in your life. As you hold onto your faith in Me, I will cause you to be stronger inside. Depend on me to incubate the promised fruit of the Holy Spirit that will soon be visible arriving just in time.

Jim, I was with you when the spring tornado hit your home in Elmwood. Trees broke through the roof. The wind howled. Rain came down in sheets. I am always there in your fury and pain even as wars and hunger curse the earth. My people often waste their lives as they become victims to forces that preventive measures would have brought peace.
I hear you and your friends and family cry out to Me. I was there in Kentucky during their flood, in Florida during Hurricane Ian. I am in Ukraine, Somalia, and every place that brings disenchantment, displacement, disillusionment, Confusion, and shattered dreams.

I want those who are kingdom citizens to walk among the poor who are starving. I want you to hear the cries of the poor. I want you to feel the pain of the homeless. Keep on in faith at the center of your world's pain.

Like My mercy, My Light falls during the storms when it is needed the most. My reality and power are things you do not understand just now. One day you will know Me directly.

I will keep you when you come to Me during storms, problem times, and your suffering. Keep traveling with Me on your journey to heavenly Zion. Pay the price of yourself, as I have paid for you. Turn the tears of weeping into springs of blessings.

I will be there right with you. Sometimes I know everything appears to be negative. Don't be afraid of the future.

Perhaps these roadblocks in your thinking refuse to go away. Brother Jim, there is hope. I totally understand where you are at this moment. I want you to move past these roadblocks.

When my children face the darkness and the storms in life, they doubt the strength of faith. I am your Savior. I provide encouragement and practical help to focus on your blessings.

Chapter Five

PRAYER AND FAITHFULNESS

Faithfulness calls us to spiritual practices in our relationship with God. The way we imagine God will determine how we live. If we see God in Jesus, we will search for a clear relationship with our creator. Prayer is expected. Like anything else faithfully completed, becomes more natural and normal.

When we become irregular for praying, we feel awkward. We do not know what we can say to God. God does not want us to wait until we can word our prayers flawlessly. God just wants us to be faithful in our prayers. Psalm 119:164. This psalm writer prayed seven time each and every day. His attitude was to be continually praised.

David, "the sweet psalmist of Israel," was just this. He was faithful in prayer. II Samuel 23:1.

Hundreds of thousands of books and articles have been written on prayer. Prayer can be complicated or simple. Faithfulness in prayer is not measured by length, flowery language, or filled with our words. "Thought" prayers or "breath" prayers start a prayerful conversation between us and God.

Prayer is the glue that holds together the relationship between God and us. The gift of prayer provides fuel for faithful living. Jesus is the best example. He lived close to the Father because he was in constant communication.

His prayers were quite natural and intimate.

Prayer as a Gracious Gift

Prayer is one of God's most gracious gifts. In prayer our weary souls are transported from darkened valleys onto the plains of our heavenly home. Prayer is an ongoing demonstration of our faith. It is not a passive act on our part. It is active ministry. Pray until something happens. We have all experienced being persistent in our prayers. Some faithful praying people have waited five, ten, or more years before they know their prayers have been answered.

Our relationship with God is initiated by God. God is seeking us. During the storms of life stir up our prayerful pleas, we do not know how to start.

Faithing is to believe God is calling on us to choose to be in a relationship. When I wrote *The Joy of Prayer: The Way to Intimacy with God*, some readers experienced an epiphany.

Seeing a sunrise, looking at a child's smile, smelling a budding flower, hearing the cry of a gull, admiring a beautiful painting, tastes of wine, hearing church bells, smelling incense, hearing a joyful whistle while we work, holding a puppy, drinking pure cold water on a hot summer's day. We are startled by how close God is. With God so close, prayer becomes easily said and heard.

In the beginning of our relationship with the Creator, we relate in polite responses, soft voices, and pious words. We try to pray and listen to God. Prayer than becomes an act of faithfulness that is grounded, expansive, and imaginative. The intimacy is such that we can rage at God. Question God. Cry out to God. Laugh with God. Push God away. Chase God. Fall in love with God. Praying in grace and faith, produces a robust intimacy between ourselves and God.

There are many ways to know God. Surprising times of startled joy comes as we see how close and easily known God is to us. With God so immediate, praying becomes easy. Our response to God is natural and sensual. Continuing in prayer, we request without ceasing. Unexpected doors will open. Matthew 7:7. Faithfulness to prayer is our key to exercising our faith.

God will listen to us. And God loves us. God is interested in everything about us. Prayer is not a tool to influence God, to change the Divine, but to change something in us through this intimate contact.

Ask for the grace of faithfulness to prayer. Even if it is poor or dry, it will place us into love and strengthen our faith. Faith determines the quality of our relationship with God. Prayer deepens the conviction that our faith touches God. Luke 11:9-13.

Read Isaiah 49:14-16.

Everything Becomes a Prayer

Everything can become prayer. I walk to stay healthy. I read the Bible to encounter Christ. I listen to music to relax. We act out of love or from responsibility for safe care.

Life reminds us that God is with us. The ugly and the broken remind us of faithing toward the promises. The beauty and the restoration illuminate the promises. Experiencing pleasure or discomfort, joy or disgust, we find God and an invitation to deepen our faithfulness to God.

Praying shifts our attention. Walking opens our senses to the presence of God. Walking makes footprints that mark peaceful joy and freedom. When we carefully read the Bible, we sense God in the text.

To understand the possibility of intimacy with God, reflect on the story of Jacob wrestling with God. Genesis 32:22-32. Jacob said that he had seen God face to face. The psalms bring examples of faithful praying. They are filled with emotions and imaginations. Fearful, angry, and willing to shout at God. Psalm 35:22-23, 138:1-2.

Psalm 43 is a prayer to God in times of darkness and trouble. The prayer asks for defense against the unjust, mourns oppression, and cries for guidance when we feel completely helpless.

The Book of Lamentations from which the hymn, "Great Is Thy Faithfulness" comes, along with Job, are helpful. Isaiah 61:1 is another. Learning new ways to pray through changing liturgy is difficult. We become comfortable about how things are. Faithing is doing something new. New experiences and experiments are opportunities for learning how to pray.

We might list teachings that are now meaningless. List those things you want to retain.

When we become exhausted, upset, out of sorts, confused, and beside ourselves, we turn our attention to breathing. This attention reminds us of the closeness of the spirit, the joy of life, and the longing of God to be in relationship with us. Prayer and faith are not separate realities.

Prayer is closely connected with the reality of faith. Prayer is the giving of ourselves in complete devotion to Christ. Faithing is to know our own helplessness. Prayer is the existential calling of our inner emptiness. Jesus' teachings are contrary to our natural tendencies that it is a paradox. Christ overturns our human concepts.

God offers incomparable benefits to those living in love. The invitation from God is an intimate relationship. In every season of our lives, Yahweh is with us. Psalm 103:1-2. We are never alone. One benefit of prayer is that we become more like Jesus. God surrounds us with immense power that is an indescribable benefit. Love has no limits.

We are not lifeless channels. With divine ecology, we enjoy the benefits of connection. Prayer changes us. We will pass into another eternal environment where love reigns. We focus on living, not dying. We give all our strength and energy in the loving work of God. We go upward into a life of joy.

Setting Souls Free to Live in Joy

Another benefit is a new revelation for setting our souls free to live in joy. From birth to death, in grow in our awareness and life itself becomes prayer. A faithful approach to prayer recognizes that God has control over our lives. We pray in response to God with gratitude for the benefits that Jesus told us about during his brief earthly ministry.

In the dark nights, we sense that our prayers have gone unanswered, or that we did not get what we expected or deserved. Focusing on ourselves, our needs, and what we must do blinds us to God's action on our behalf. An intimate prayer life with benefits shows we are not God. God acts with grace as Jesus invited us to pray. The Holy Spirit empowers us. Our prayer is our response to God being God.

As we read the Bible, an image of God will form inside us. Prayerful meditation of the Bible will teach us about the love of God. God loves us incessantly. God is love. Encountering Christ, who is present in the Word of God will help us discover God in the world. John 4:14, 7:37-39. The Bible overturns human concepts.

Jesus was awaited for thousands of years. His coming oriented towards the seeking of the one who would be our redemption. After a long period of expectation, he came into the world. For more than 30 years, Jesus led a secluded life, far from the activity expected of a Messiah. Multitudes continue waiting. Humankind was confused. People thought that Christ, who was so completely unified with God, did not need to pray.

Faithfulness is our joyful response to the grace-filled initiative that God has already taken for us. God is in charge before we pray, when we pray, and after we pray. With our eyes of faith, we understand that the more suppressed we are with personal activities, the more time we must spend praying. If not, we will become empty. Carrying water in a sieve will not work. Not that we have no faith. Our faith is small. Everything depends on God. If God gives you strength for including us in the divine work, it does not mean that any of us is irreplaceable.

God will manage with or without us. God does not need human intervention. God holds the fate of the world in divine hands. If we do not pray, no one will need us. Empty souls are of no use. Authentic action is born in prayer. Praying is a sign and indication of our closeness or our distance from God. Prayer is an expression of our bond with God.

We feel good when we feel the presence of God. Praying becomes something appealing to us. Once we begin experiencing a time of dryness in prayer, we cannot afford the temptation to resign our prayer work.

Faith is a decisive influence on what we pray for and the intensity of our praying.

Faith changes our mentality and charges us for more intensity. Our praying will become more and more subordinate to the work of the Holy Spirit. Romans 8:26-27. We must put God first. We must not resign from our own pace and effort. Leave all concern for ourselves and for the results of our actions to God whose will is to give us boundless love.

Simplified Ways of Praying

God desires us to simplify our ways of praying. We include more listening. We do not need to use words. Spend time just thinking. Think like Jesus thinks. Think about how Jesus loves you. Jesus loves those that you love. That assurance will give us peace. With a person who is close, silence will not bring an uncomfortable distance. Jesus wants us to be able to calm ourselves before him. We can simply look at him. Just as we can pray with our words and thoughts, we can pray with silence. We do not have to exert ourselves to express anything with words. God knows that we are smiling and why we are. Smiles toward God express joy flowing from genuine praying.

As children of God, we have the benefit of instant intimacy. The calendar of God is always open to us. God gives us full attention. Proverbs 15:8.
The more we come into the presence of God, the more natural and comfortable we will be. God desires our intimacy and fellowship. God loves and enjoys being with us. Psalm 145:18.

God will be God. As God's daughters and sons, our faithing prayer response enables us to live closer to the example of Jesus. Jesus invites us to prayer because of the benefits with which he gifts us. Psalm 103:2.

Jesus has done many unbelievable works, more than could be written down in a billion books. John 21:25. Solidarity with God and other people and our joy are beneficial beyond number.

Prayer life cannot be sustained without intention and effort. Faithfulness in prayer requires attention, time, interest, and commitment. Nothing draws us to God and God to us like prayer. Psalm 34:18, 145:8.

Praying gives attention to ourselves as well as God. Our capacity for discernment is strengthened. Our thankfulness makes us more pleasing and content. This connection evokes meeting needs, sharing life's burdens, and celebrating joys. We discover and rediscover our need for God, our need for others, and their need for us. Appropriate humility in our faithing is another benefit. We seek to imitate Jesus in love.

Faithfulness and Unity

Prayer unites us to all people who are seeking to follow Jesus. Prayer draws us to God. It draws God to us. Praying eyes see Jesus close-up. Faithfulness involves praying for and with another in the presence of God. Faith increases the intimacy as the will and purpose of God.

We experience God through a variety of images that help in our opportunities to relate to God. Spontaneous joy, openness to new ways of being. Revealing more and more of ourselves becomes deeper and deeper s God relates to us in new and surprising ways. Faithing is in the stillness may not be clear and comfortable. Even one new insight brings effective intimate prayers.

My niece, Amy McReynolds, lives in Belfast, Northern Ireland. In the sanctuary of the church, there is an old Irish blessing that relates to faithfulness in prayer.

"God with me, God before me, God behind me, God in me, God beneath me, God above me. God on my right and God on my left, God when I lie own God when I sit down, God when I arise, God in the heart of everyone who thinks of me, God in the mouth of everyone who speaks of me, God in every eye that sees me, God in every ear that hears me."

Sallie McFague, noted professor at Vanderbilt University Divinity School, encourages us to think about where God is, by naming the world as our meeting place with God. The way we meet God in the world is through our relationship and interdependence with all creatures on earth. Her theological model suggests that "God is closer to us than we are to ourselves, because God is the breath or spirit that gives life to the billions of different bodies that make up God's body. God is also the source, power, and goal of everything that is, for the creation depends utterly on God." Sallie McFague, *The Body of God: An Ecological Theology*, p. viii)

My life journey is not in isolation. It involves every human that ever lived on earth. We are all interlocked with all our ancestors. Who I am today is helped or hindered by people who existed before me.

Prayer is our best tool for caring for others. We are all a part of the same family. That is the reason we pray, "Our Father." Matthew 6:9. We share common needs. That is why we pray about "our bread." Matthew 6:11- 13.

We all share in an identity with Christ. Praying takes us to a place that makes living faith our unmatched focus. Our secret place keeps us alert to God. We are different as Christ lives inside us. Praying keeps us attuned to our transformed identity as the foundation for how we strive to live. Jesus often showed his love for his followers through prayer. Jesus knew Peter's faith would be threatened by the events that would come. He told Peter, "I have prayed for you, that your faith should not fail." Luke 22:32.

Catching the wind on the wings of prayer, church came together in one accord. Acts 1:14. As a result, challenges were met, and faithful believers were emboldened. They broke out of their cocoons to see the needs of others.

Prayer lifts our minds out of the mundane and muddy times. In grace our hearts rejoice. We respect God's holiness. We really want to be better.

God wakes up every eternal seed planted in our souls. While we are rooted in this earth, in this time, place, and space, a part of heaven will blossom into this beautiful reality. We will discuss heaven in chapter ten.

We cherish the moments when Yahweh touches our lives with the coming of the morning sun giving us a glimpse of the eternal. We are determined to show love. To pray is to love. To love is to pray.

The prayer that continues to guide my spiritual journey is "Make Me an Instrument of Thy Peace." It is attributed to Saint Francis of Assisi, whose time on earth was dated from the years 1181-1226.

"Lord, make me an instrument of thy peace,
Where there is hatred, let me sow love.
When there is injury, pardon.
Where there is doubt, faith.
Where there is despair, hope.
Where there is darkness, light.
Where there is sadness and joy.

O divine Master, grant that I may not so much seek
To be consoled as to console,
To be understood as to understand,
To be loved as to love.
For it is in giving that we receive.
It is in pardoning that we are pardoned.
It is in dying to self that we are born into eternal life."

My praying friend, I love to hear your prayers. You bring all of who you are, all of who you have been, and all of who you are becoming into our relationship. I listen to your prayers in your secret place or as an important part of worship. I listen closely to your pastoral prayers, the hymns and songs, your affirmations of faith, and your prayers of confession.

Prayer is My gift as the act of reaching out to Me in faith. Prayer is a gift that you can share with others. Ask for My blessings. My son Jesus slipped away many times so that he could pray. He felt that prayer was necessary for staying in touch will My will.

I know Jesus prayed continuously. He had much to pray about, and so do you. Jim, read John 17, the prayer Jesus prayed during Jesus and his disciples last meal together before his arrest and the crucifixion.

During that last meal, Jesus washed the disciples' feet as a symbol of his coming to be a servant.

You are now walking on the same pathways that I walk. Prayer is the moving and walking with Me. I, too, enjoy that prayer etched into the Northern Irish churches as a guide.

I was with you in the Blue Ridge Mountains and on the walking trails near your home, and the beaches from North Carolina to California. Walk lightly as you age, attending to each step. My faithful walker, imagine that each time your foot touches the ground, you are deepening your relationship with Me.

Some people use My gift of prayer is used for the wrong purpose. A folk is a wonderful tool for eating food, but it is a disappointing method for drinking water. I sense your discouragement because you are trying to use it to accomplish the wrong objective. Your prayers must radiate from your heart that desires My glory more than comfort. Luke 1:38. When your desires line up with heaven's goals, prayer is touching My power. My gift of prayer will soothe your anxieties, help you escape temptations, and secures My forgiveness when you fail. My gift will strengthen your legs for living in Me and for loosening your tongue to speak faithfully of Me.

Chapter Six

WRITING AND FAITHFULNESS

In a prayerful mood, I walked across the field through Elmwood Park on this icy December morning. My job is being in a rhythm of walking and writing. Writing books is a great pleasure for me. I feel anointed to dive deep into a question. I share my own experience for the benefit of others who are walking along faithfully with me. Being a writer has open doors to many opportunities I had never imagined.

Writing has been a large part of my ministry. As a teenager, I published my first book, *Children in My Heart*. Because of my writing gifts, I was given many opportunities for faithfulness to God.

Many religious writers or ministers who major in the ministry of writing stagger us by the size of their prolific output. We are surprised by the quality of their work. They never suffer from overmuch writing. Their writing gets better with each attempt to write.

It is a bit humbling to spend ministry time writing. There is no choir of voices in my writing office. Writing lacks the exhilaration of public preaching. There is no stain-glassed window. Few will tell a writer what an amazing book she has written. Writing ministry is lonely, hidden, and unappreciated. An ordained ambassador for Christ finds it easier to be recognized when standing in a pulpit or on-stage preaching.

I direct spiritual writing retreats to encourage others in their writing. I appreciate that faithful writing is so much more than religious writing. Christian books are not always helpful.

And like writing, doing psychotherapy or counseling in the dead of the night with a couple threatening to abandon their marriage than when a minister sits at a desk alone. James L. Sullivan, president of the Sunday School Board of the Southern Baptist Convention emphasized, "Writing is a ministry, and it is a highly important one." He was an ordained Southern Baptist preacher whose ministry was to serve as head man for the largest producer of Christian literature on the planet.

Writing has exciting possibilities. It has so many growing points. People honor me by saying they quoted from my books. Writing calls for more than we have with more thinking, more reading, more prayer, and more literary craftsmanship.

The Christian writer is a teacher, an analyst, a prophet, a comforter, and a conscience. Many well-known and brilliant pastors felt it an honor to serve Christ at the denominational headquarters. These women and men were called with something of a divine perspective and a special anointing. The hand of God rested upon the shoulder of Christian writers.

With divine accreditation, the writing ministry transfers the power and glory from the vital relationship with God to the printed page.

This growing ministry is heightened by the urgent need on the part of lay and clergy leaders to discharge their teaching. Most Protestant Christians are in the house of God for only one hour on Sunday.

Writing Reaches People

Most people define writing narrowly. Many loathed to even call themselves writers. Charles Allen, famous Methodist pastor, noted that he had reached more people from his published books than his lifetime of preaching. Thousands of preachers would say the same thing about their writing.

Faithful writing has intent and purpose fueled by a pull to love, care, and do more. Faithful writers experience eruptions of surprise, randomness, and synchronicity stirring within.

Ideas come as a writer prays, sleeps at night, or bubbles in the mind while lathering in soapsuds in the shower.

When I pray in my home, I hear chimes ring out songs such as "Great Is Thy Faithfulness" from the Saint Paul United Methodist Church in Elmwood. The bells ring out the hours. The sounds remind us of the passing of time. The hours chime predictably and reliably. The sounds of chimes remind me of the love and faithfulness of God. Palm 89:2.

Faithfulness is necessary when the promises of God seem to contradict what we are seeing now. Faith is the opposite of fear. It protects us from fear of worldly troubles.

Pray that our faithful writing allows us to draw closer to the more complete reality of our existence. God allows difficult situations to take place.

If you write, you are a writer. But are you a faithful writer? Faithful writing has to do with intent and purpose. When our writing has to do with a call to God and is fueled by miracles. Google "Books by James E. McReynolds," you will find thousands of bookstores throughout the world that are selling my books. Even if I do not profit from their sales, I am being faithful by touching the world.

Writers have ideas bubble up in our heads as we lather on the soapsuds during a shower. Writers read a passage so inspiring that we grab our notebooks and immediately write down our thoughts. Writers wake up in the middle of the night with something they know they must do. Writers experience unusual things like a yellow butterfly landing on the hand that Is interpreted as a sign.

Lyrics of songs give a plot idea. The sight is so vivid that we race to find a pen and paper to capture it before it disappears from the mind.

When the action we feel inspired to take after eruptions of randomness, synchronicity, or a joy full surprise cause us to write or type words, we are faithful writers. Writing with an inner urge and an inspiration makes a faithful writer.

Be faithful as a steward of your writing talent. Matthew 25:21, 23. We relate more to the "little" than the faithfulness aspect. We are not in control of how much talent we have been blessed with. We can choose how we use his talent.

Faithful writers put their faith into writing. They follow God's leading. Every time we sit down to write, we choose where to focus. We act on the topic we are writing about. I was a prolific writer when I served at the Sunday School Board of the Southern Baptist Convention. I prayed every time I was assigned to write a news article for Baptist Press or any other writing task.

Faithing writers find partners with whom we can both give and receive encouragement and love. Faith trusts in God's timing. One letter separates the word writing from waiting. The two join together. Like me, sometimes we are hurled into a dark storm if we lose a cherished manuscript on our computer. God is still in control.

As I do a lot of heavy travel in my preaching tours, I feel extremely exhausted. There are times when I just can't write. I just don't feel like writing in those dark days. This mood creates an inner resentment against my work and at times a too prolific style. There may come days that a writer will be unproductive.

My wife and friends use me to help in their writing. At Carson-Newman College, I wrote love notes and words in cards for the young men to send to their girlfriends. They called me the poet laureate of Memorial Hall.

We can help others succeed in their writing tasks in individuals meetings, coaching, lectionary sermon writing groups, or book clubs.

Steps of faith follow the guidance of God who has inspired some mighty writers. Journal ways God has been good to you. Collect moments of God's faithfulness, keeping them tucked away to look on in the moments of disbelief or doubt with joy. Slow down, take a deep breath, and connect with your shadow. Struggling to write faithfully, I talk to my inner shadow. Finding the willpower leads to procrastination and avoidance.

How can we do faithful writing when we are tired? After talking to your shadow, start your timer and write for just fifteen minutes.

When your time is up, hug yourself. The mental work of writing has physical consequences. When the builders were constructing our new home in Elmwood, they told me how exhausted they were by the end of their day. A writer faces the same phenomena a builder struggles with trying to maneuver a joist into place.

Writing Brings Exhaustion

That is how our bodies work. Our hearts will beat rapidly. Producing adrenaline, sweat rolls down our faces whether the cause of the stress is physical or mental.

The kinds of writing stress we face includes having hundreds of pages of notes but no idea how to get started. We leave our writing to the last minute. We doubt that we'll finish the 1,500 required words in the time remaining. These kinds of stresses wear us out, just as much as if we have been performing physical work. Our brains use a disproportionate amount of oxygen. That is one reason I am required to use a C-pap machine. Muscles that are moving require oxygen. Of course, the brain is not an organ, but the point still holds true.

So, next time you spend a day doing significant writing, don't be surprised when you feel exhausted. Writers should drink lots of water ss you work at your desk. I try to drink a large glass of water as soon as I wake up. There have been times when I look after an hour or so, and I have had only a sip of my water. Even mild dehydration can lead to anger, mood swings, and fatigue. Drink plenty of water. This habit forces me to get up and use the bathroom. Writers should get up and stretch every hour. We will find that we are more productive. If we have to walk to work, this will give you a daily exercise.

Another good time for a walk is after lunch or supper. This helps with indigestion and improves blood sugar. Every time I see my medical doctor, he asks me to walk.

Take up some sport: tennis, swimming, golfing. Join a gym. Work out three times each week.

Faithful writing is never easy. It is tiring and demanding. People are surprised just how difficult it is. The same goes for preaching sermons. No wonder we feel so much anxiety when we share the Word of God.

For me, writing is worth doing and it is part of what makes my life worth living. Nobody wants to waste their life. Ordained ministers who write well choose to devote all their time to writing. Writing is a good ministry after retirement. If anyone tries to tell you that writing is a wasted life, do not listen. Write and keep writing. See where it leads. We carefully write our sermons, but preaching is a differing media s we ask God to go with us into the pulpit. We will remember the essential things, and sometimes we speak spontaneously ideas that we have read or heard that completes the sermon delivery. Frederick Buechner is a preacher who has chosen to write. The Presbyterians have not taken his ordination status away just because he has no appointment or call to preach. He has written eleven novels. He has written non-fiction books. His novel *Godric* won a Pulitzer Prize.

Writing and preaching are two different forms of communication. The first is marked by permanence, the second by immediacy. The test of faithful writing is not the same as the test for faithful preaching. Immediacy of apprehension and response is necessary. (Henry Grady Davis, *Design for Preaching*, p. 265)

A listener cannot see the visible markings, commas, capitals and periods. He can only go by the sounds she or he hears, the expressions seen, and the movements of the preacher. There is nothing else for understanding and interpreting. There is no going back and rereading.

Any writer who stays faithful and shows up to write will discover she can look over her life with satisfaction and joy. Stay faithful. Keep showing up. Keep writing faithfully.

God calls us by many names. Writers have come up with a long list of the names we call God: Lord God Almighty, beloved Savior, divine gift of grace, precious bridegroom, rose of Sharon, sweet comforter, lily of the valley, defender and deliverer, Prince of Peace, my soul's desire, Alpha and Omega, King of Heaven, Son of Man, my soul's release, the great I am, Ancient of days, Jehovah Jireh, Messiah, Breath of Heaven, Bright and morning star, Light and Life, El Shaddai, Hope of Glory, Thou Most High, Living Water, Bread of Life, Gate of Heaven, Root of David, Promised Savior, High Tower, Returning King, Life and Resurrection, the Great True Vine, Lion of Judah, Chief Cornerstone, Great High Priest, Good Shepherd, Lamb of God, and an unending of names unlimited by faithful writers.

The world praises quick results. Ours might be slow in coming. Writing is heavy and hard work. I write to give readers some joy, hope, love, and faithful endurance. I pray my books will remind them that they are not alone. God is good. There is hope. I believe my writing gets better as I trust God. I pray God is the writer. When I preach, I ask God to take over the pulpit and the words I say.

Writing Improves with Each Book

My writing has improved with each book. My style and storytelling give out a joy. I am proud of everything that I have accomplished. Recently, I have worked with amazing people and a faithful publisher.

The work has taken a heavy toll on my mental, spiritual, and physical health. My wife Laurel keeps asking me, "When are you going to get away from your intense ministry of writing?"

She speaks out of her love and concern. As I see the news of bookstores all around the world, I realize God is using me to bring joy to people. Still at times, I think I can never be enough.

My wife says that I had way too much work for one person. There are other issues, but I don't want to share all that now.

We get only one life. My life must have enough room for my writing as minister of joy. I do not know what my future holds, but I know with faith that it will be graced in the Supreme Creator.

Living in faithfulness, Christ gradually becomes a light that shines during our whole lives. Every single moment of life brings us the Presence. Grace loves us all. John 3:16. Grace is the expression of love. Every moment is linked to that love. Everything we experience is tied to the love of God who loves us.

Faith traces God in everything. It brings security and peace. Our confidence is immerse in love. Faith's peace is beyond understanding. In reality we remain uneasy and anxious. The heart will cause us to be restless like a moth beating against a light bulb. We hold a distorted image of God. We then fear God.

Giving ourselves completely to God is the highest form of reliance. Faith is the process of accepting the redeeming action of Christ. (Ernest Boyer, *A Way in the World: Family Life as a Spiritual Discipline*, pp. 4-23)

God blesses faithfulness. Faithfulness develops faith. This fruit of the Spirit insists on the exercise of faith. We become stronger with time. Faithfulness produces fruit. Colossians 2:6-7.

Faithfulness proves the reality of God. Consistent exercise of faith despite setbacks, sends out a message that God will sustain us as we follow Christ. Acts 16:29-30. Faithfulness builds relationships within the church community. Hebrews 10:25.

My servant, I gave you the gift of writing to bring joy to the world. Faithful writers give an epiphany of light when darkness falls into your life.

I know that sometimes writing the right word is like blundering along searching for a flashlight only to find the batteries are dead. My anointed scribe, the light of my grace, my love, and my joy will be with you even in the dry and dark days when your creative juices refuse to flow as you sit in front of your computer.

Let My Light burst through and warm the world. I am the Word that is in Me and shared with you. James, your sermons and books have been used to help people understand My Gospel.

You have managed to throw open fresh new windows on the ancient writings. Scripture comes alive as communicators use My gifts, and other seekers get a whole new perspective by My hands used by your hands as a way I can show up. Faith and culture need your work as a meeting place.

I created you in my image. I give you My peace, grace, and love so that with My Spirit, you can interpret Me in My reflection. As a citizen of My Kingdom, your work will contribute the bringing My children closer, to reconciling enemies, to bring more respectful dialogue between diverse cultures.

You are a part of the human search for meaning. I do want your work to be used in reflection and conversation to pride a focus for living My message, My Good News, in each day. My Spirit will enable you to help people in your contemporary culture, see My Light.

I have consoled you in the death of your brother David. I give you your life and hope. My biggest commandment is for you and your people to love one another. That is the way you arise into a new life.

Continue your faithfulness. Jim, be constant and persevering in communicating your thoughts and desires to Me.

I want you to step out in faith. I realize that for you, faith seems like jumping into the unknown.

Take a leap on My behalf. That's what faithfulness is all about.

Chapter Seven

PREACHING AND FAITHFULNESS

"The highest service than men may attain to on earth is to preach the Word of God," wrote John Wyclif. I have a framed copy of my office wall to see every day when I am tempted to curb my preaching face to face in or out of season. I have known the joys and heartaches of a preacher. I have been privileged by the delight of a huge audience and the despondency of empty pews.

I have lived through rapid changes in the church. Some have been caused by rapid changes in the culture. I continue to preach because it is part of my faithfulness. The darkening shadows of the total church picture cause preachers to lose enthusiasm.

There are times when we enter the pulpit feeling anxious and below par. The eagerness of the congregation lifted me up. Congregations differ. The sermon that is the height of joy for one church sounds dead to another.

Each congregation holds differing worlds of thought. There is a wide gap between preacher and congregation. That gulf has robbed preaching of much of its power. Impatient people value the sermon not by its quality, but by its brevity.

After 70 years of preaching, I often ask, "Did my sermons help you? Did you learn any things from me as your pastor?" Some said sermons are not really helpful. Some reasons ere triteness of content, poor language, poor organization, lack of balance between heart and head.

Preaching effective sermons is an impossible duty. Few wait in anticipation for the next sermon to hear. Most said they learned most about faith through the words of hymns.

Today's congregation has increased leisure time. When I accepted an appointment to a church, I expected that my primary role would that of a preacher. Mu lengthy an expensive training at universities and theological seminary was my preparation. This gave content for sermons. I expected to have a church in which to preach. Until recent years, people attended church.

We are illusioned to think that a preacher who ministers successfully to one segment of culture can have equal success with others. It is difficult to be "all things to all men. Individual preachers reach certain types more effectively than others.

"Go Where the Joy Is"

A faithful minister may spend a lifetime searching for a church ministry where she or he is most suited.

The gospel of Jesus Christ is a proclaimed gospel. A sermon is not really a sermon until it is shared with the congregation. A minister is never a preacher until it is communicated with others. The lowest attendance for a sermon is two people. On 17 occasions, I know I have preached to only one. At Warich Chapel in Saint Joseph State Hospital, I delivered a sermon to one person in the substance abuse unit. Blazing new trials in planting a new church sometimes attracted only one listener.

I still believe in the power and necessity of preaching. It is vitally important for our souls. II Timothy 4:2. Faithless preaching insists on performance, illustrations for entertainment, drama, and theatrics.

By faith and brazen faithfulness, I never missed preaching one sermon. As for losing my book manuscript, I think this one is better.

The most polished manuscript is never a sermon. It is preparation. Phillips Brooks has two large statues of himself in the Christ Church in Boston. Brooks reminds us that preaching is both truth and personality. (Phillips Brooks, *Lectures on Preaching*, p. 5)

Nothing changes lives for God than faithful preaching. When we put ourselves under the preaching of God's Word, it is one of the precious few moments in modern life when we button our lip, resist the temptation to respond immediately, and focus our energy and attention on hearing with faith. Paul expected Timothy to preach faithfulness. II Timothy 4:2- 5.

"With preaching Christianity stands or falls." (Clyde Reid, *The Empty Pulpit*, p. 34) To preach is to preach the Word of God. To preach is to speak with authority. The preacher is called "a herald of God." James Stewart, *A Herald of God*. She may be called "a servant of the Word." H.H. Farmer, *The Servant of the Word*.

Karl Barth wrote: "On Sunday morning when the bells ring to call he congregation and its minister to church, there is in the air an expectancy that something great, crucial, and even momentous to happen." (Karl Barth, *The Word of God and the Word of Man*, p. 104.)

Effective preaching helps us in the faithfulness of life-giving self-forgetfulness. Preaching exposes our sin. It challenges us to change. Being occupied with nothing but me. At the sermon's climax, we are captivated by Christ.

Henry Ward Beecher was approached by a young divinity student who was troubled that she planned to enter ministry. What was his worry was is just how long he will need to prepare a sermon. Beecher told him, "I have been preparing to preach since I was born. For the life of a faithful preacher, every moment is a preparation. Every book you read, every encounter he has with people and places contributes to preaching." Helmut Thielicke, a German pastor, said, "Every conversation I engage in becomes at bottom a meditation, a preparation, a gathering of material for my preaching. I can no longer listen with disinterest even to a play in the theater without relating it to my pulpit. This life in all its daily involvements, becomes for me a thesaurus in which I keep rummaging because it is full of relevant material for my message."

Listening to people primes a dry pump. With demands from everywhere, preachers discover that they have no particular sermon. They must go back to the people to hear again their agony, to feel with them deeply, to become sensitive. Pastors then return to their study or their quiet place with God.

To be faithful, our preaching and worship must be done purposely, not haphazardly. God is a God of order. Isaiah describes a vision he experienced in the temple. It happened the year Uzziah died of leprosy. The holiness of God was revealed. Isaiah 6:3 and 6:5.

God is adored. All too frequently our cleansing and absolution have been omitted in churches in the free church tradition. Contemplating the holiness of God awakens our sense of sin and forgiveness.

Music plays a part in this. Lay reading of the preacher's text and the faithfully prepared sermon are in juxtaposition for the joy of the Lord. The congregation responds to the grace of God. "Here am I! Send me!"

John Knox, the preacher who was founder of the Church of Scotland, preached from his window of his Edinburgh home. The author felt an amazing joy as he imagined Knox preaching the gospel. John 5:11, Acts 13:52, I John 1:4.

The churches in the 2020's does not appear to experience the joy and exuberance that the early churches did. Worship has been misunderstood as a dull, sober, and doleful rather than a faithful relationship with our creator full of festivity, celebration, and joy. (Ronald A. Ward, *Worship: The New Testament Basis*, pp. 364-365)

John Knox spoke of his own reaction: "Adoration and thanksgiving, confrontation with God's will, confession of sin, the seeking of forgiveness and other help we need, affirmation of faith, consecration of life." (John Knox, *The Integrity of Preaching*, New York: Harper and Row, p. 78)

Faith makes a preacher believable. Absence of faith can't be disguised. Authority gives a preacher the right to speak. Authority may mean ordination, a call, a talent and educational preparation.

When I wrote *The Joy of Preaching*, my passion, enthusiasm, and joy of preaching oozed out. I have proceeded to write and teach preaching with the assumption that preaching is neither wholly human nor wholly divine. God calls a dedicated human being, fills that person with the Holy Spirit, and uses me to communicate the gospel.

Every faithful textbook on preaching states that preaching without the Holy Spirit is dead. The Spirit inspires preparation, grants unction in delivery, and produces all significant results that follow the preaching event.

John Knox said, "True preaching from start to finish is the work of the Holy Spirit. Without the Holy Spirit, there is no church. Communication of the gospel is a message shared in the inspiration of the Holy Spirit.

Writing and Preaching Are Related

Writing and preaching are related. James Stewart, professor of preaching at New College, the seminary of the University of Edinburgh, insisted that regardless of the method of delivery, must begin by writing out sermons. The faithful preacher, undaunted in determination will continue to improve her mode of expression. If she reads and rereads her sermon, it begins to run through the juices of her personality.

John Henry Jowett wrote: "No sermon is ready for preaching nor for writing out, until we can express its theme in a short, pregnant sentence as clear as a crystal. I find that the getting of that sentence the hardest, most exacting and the most labor in my study. To compel oneself to fashion that sentence, to dismiss every word that is vague, ragged, ambiguous, to think oneself through to a form of words which defines the theme with scrupulous exactness. This is surely the most vital and essential factors in making a sermon. I do not think that any sermon ought to be preached or even written, until that sentence has emerged clear and lucid as a cloudless morning. (John Henry Jowett, *The Preacher: His Life and Work*, p. 133)

During the more than twenty years that I served as president of the Bess Streeter Aldrich Foundation, I would spend time at the Aldrich home in Elmwood reading my sermons over and over when visitors were not present for a tour. My sermons would flow and felt natural. I entered the sanctuary with expectation and with dependence on the Holy Spirit. Careful preparation leaves a bit of the joy and excitement, the product of faithfulness. (William L. Malcomson, *The Preaching Event*, pp. 101-104)

Modern ordination, or the fact that the preacher "preaches the Word," or has "sound doctrine," does not mean that the proclaimer is automatically invested in unfaithful distortions. Faithfulness in preaching means a knowledge of what is happening now. Terrorism, dictatorships, unjust wars such as in Ukraine, pandemics, bribery, rights, strikes, weather events, uncontrolled climate, 9-11, and lack of respect are present day things to be aware of.

Faithless Preaching and Distorting Truth

Faithless preaching distorts truth. It procrastinates. It fails to do the best preparation. It fails to credit other people's materials. It preaches for personal glory, prestige, power, and money. Faithless preaching avoids unpleasant subjects. It avoids audience feedback. Jesus had some words about false prophets. Matthew 7:15-20. Jesus gave harsh criticisms of the scribes and Pharisees, and the scribes. Matthew 7:15-20, Matthew 12:34- 37.

Faithfulness of the Christian preacher is demanded in Holy Scripture. Isaiah 6:5-7. The apostle Paul demanded high ministerial standards. I Timothy 3:1-7, Titus 1:5-9.

Harry Emerson Fosdick wrote, "It takes more than a preacher alone in the pulpit to make an effective sermon. If, however, the people can be there, so the sermon is not a dogmatic dialogue but a cooperative dialogue in which the congregation's objectives, questions, doubts, and confirmations are fairly stated and dealt with, something worthwhile is likely to happen." (Harry Emerson Fosdick, *The Living of These Days: An Autobiography*, p. 97)

Faithful preaching avoids legalism. Legalism is more of an attitude rather than a doctrine. Kyle Haselden defined legalism: "Christian legalism assumes that in the teachings of Jesus and his disciples, in the ten commandments, and in the elaboration of these teachings and commandments, we have a detailed, inflexible, always appropriate moral code which in its minute prescriptions, is adequate for all times, places, persons, and circumstances. (Kyle Haselden, *Morality and the Mass Media*, p. 12)

Jesus excoriated the Pharisees for such legal action. Haselden listed some reasons why legalism fails. Legalism externalizes morality. It describes the good life in restrictive and static terms. It concentrates on trivialities. It binds the future. Legalism precludes the Holy Spirit. (Ibid., pp. 15-20)

Manipulation and Faithless Preaching

The invitation to receive Christ and to be converted can smack of unfaithful preaching. A pastor may instruct members of her church to scatter throughout the audience. They are to move out of their pews, a few at a time, toward the altar or the front of the church sanctuary as the pastor gave the invitation.

The purpose was to suggest to the unconverted and initiated that people were responding to the invitation. This manipulation was to have people to be comfortable to join them. This is a delusion and is questionable for faithful preaching. Extending an invitation to a congregation to respond to the challenge of the sermon is an act of faith as long as it is not based on unethical tricks.

Some congregations demand that preachers to extend an invitation at the end of every sermon whether the unconverted are present or not. The invitation then loses any significance in the minds of the hearers. This is a mark of unfaithful preaching.

I could write another book on unfaithfulness in preaching. Distorting the truth is an area where a preacher tones down or softens the truth. Some give "white lies." They stack evidence in their favor. Interpretation of the Bible involves violating the context or reading into the text or spiritualizing.

Unfaithful preachers appeal to tradition, authority, majority opinion, prejudices, and what the crowd wants to hear. They preach for personal power, glory, prestige on things they do not believe or fail to practice. Bluffing through when not prepared. Acting as an authority in a field where the preacher is not an authority. Name dropping to impress listeners. Other unfaithful preaching involves personal preparation. Some avoid or procrastinate preparation. Depending on God to put words in their mouths. Using other people's sermons without giving credit. Overgeneralization. Unsound or false statistics. Avoiding audience feedback. Using psychological pressures. Singling people out.

In my book, *The Joy of Preaching*, I address the mystery of God calling ordinary humans to speak the Word of God. Isaiah 6:5. The faithful preacher gives people a bigger picture of God. II Corinthians 4:5. They will know God loves them immensely. The faithful preacher plays a critical role in bringing her listeners back to the center despite media messages.

It takes time to prepare. Discipline is absolutely necessary. In some of my churches I have been blessed to have a secretary employed by the congregation. She enabled me to maintain privacy and to my prayer life and a setting for study and preparation of sermons. Some naïve people use the axiom, "The Lord will provide." God will provide, but on the condition that the preacher be faithful and unremitting in sermon preparation.

My friend and mentor Dr. John Killinger commented, "When you take the pulpit to deliver the Word you were ordained to preach, let it be a real Word, and not something compounded in fever Saturday night to be delivered in spasms on Sunday morning." (John Killinger, *The Centrality of Preaching in the Total Task of the Ministry*, p. 29)

"The prima donna of the pulpit considers the worship with its appropriate mood music and lighting devices as no more than a proper setting for his moment on the stage he liturgical fanatic retreats into the astatic to escape the terrible discipline of preaching and becomes little more than the manipulation of exotic rituals." (Lycurgus M. Starkey, *The Holy Spirit at Work in the Church*, p. 80)

A frequent fault is the so-called preacher's tone. It's like a ministerial melody. The preacher has a habitual pitch tone. Some preachers serving in the Blue Ridge Mountains give a big huff after every sentence. They told me that some well-known country preachers were sick and had to huff. Today, they just huff.

Some ways to be ready to preach include running a mile. Playing the piano. They find ways to burn off excess energy to be their best selves in the pulpit.

The ultimate goal of preaching is not transformation of information It is not data exchange. It is behavioral change. Preaching is done for a change in attitudes and beliefs expressed verbally and non-verbally. Preaching calls for radical transformation.

The Bible requires Holy Spirit direction. II Timothy 2:15. Preaching may attract a crowd that applauses the preacher. Faithful preaching is true to the text. True to the whole counsel of God. God uses that kind of preaching. If the preaching is faithful, it is clear and understandable. This means the preacher pays attention to the flow, the structure, the pace, and the length of sermons. Congregations must know what the text was about and what she was trying to say. Preaching's unique claim to a hearing is that it is the Word of God. Resting in scripture as authority is an act of faith.

No Preaching Is Unbiblical

There is no preaching that is not biblical. Preachers commissioned by the church and called by God have settled for secondary utterances. God expects faithfulness in our preaching while people are crying out, not simply for dealing with the unimportant, but seeking a clear Word from God.

One who preaches must speak the revealed Word of God. She must be faithful to her preaching to what God has given in the Bible. Paul instructed Timothy not to just preach, but to "preach the Word." This is the content of our preaching. Preaching explains the Word of God, and nothing else. It is difficult because human beings do not want to listen to the Word from God. It is offensive. In the New Testament we find that Paul and the apostles were persecuted and imprisoned and killed because they preached.

Preaching does something. Isaiah 55:10. Faithful preaching bears fruit. Preaching is like the rain that falls down and brings the seeds and flowers in the springtime of faith. Jeremiah said the Word was like a fire or a hammer that breaks hard rocks. That is the Word of God. Hebrews 4:12.

The realization of the Word of God is required in everyday life. It is life flowing from faith. Encountering the Word, we regard the text as impersonally, as an object to be examined, or an aid for finding a solution for a problem. Another way is to see it personally, as a subject. The text becomes for us a mystery. If our intention in reading the Bible is to acquire more knowledge, you think of it as an object.

The Holy Scripture is an inspired text. Our relation to the text should be personal. Christ is present as we study a text. We encounter a living Christ through the gift of faith. Reading the Bible is a fundamental factor of our faithfulness and the sharing in the life of God. God gives us a revelation of the divine through the intercession of the scripture. Our intense contact with Christ Jesus, who is present in his Word will enable us to identify with him even more.

The words recorded in the New Testament are expressions of the mystery of his Presence. The unimaginable Presence requires our openness and in time, our transformation into Christ. The purpose of our living our time on earth will be finished. Our faith will then reach its fullness.

I have written about authority problems in unfaithful preaching. It is easily abused. Jesus spoke with authority. Matthew 7:28-29. Faithful preachers declare the truth with boldness. Faithful preachers are authentic. Their unique personality will pour out. She is comfortable in her own skin. She connects with her congregation.

Dress and appearance matters. Appearance enhances communication. If listeners are drawn to the appearance of the preacher, the attire is inappropriate. Women who wear sexy mini-skirts and expose their body are inappropriate in their dress. This is simplified by a minister who wears a robe.

I wear a robe, a classy black one with doctoral bars on the sleeves. I wear a stole that exposes the season of the year. I have one with JOY sewed into it as I am anointed as the minister of joy to the world. The robe was given to me in 1972 by Southminster United Presbyterian Church in Nashville for completion of my doctor's degree at Vanderbilt Divinity School. Wearing a robe is like a doctor or nurse, police, fire, or military persons distinguish themselves by wearing a uniform.

One distraction for listeners is wearing a crooked tie or wearing socks that droop, revealing bare legs. "I hate to see a big hairy leg hanging out," a parishioner noted. Buy dark socks that will not creep down the calf to the ankle.

Authentic Preaching Affects Eternity

Authentic preaching is full of passion. It is an advocate for Christ. These qualities are indispensable for faithful preaching. Preaching is teaching. Teaching is a gift. The book of James gives admonitions about speech. James reminds his readers that those who teach the Word of God are held to a higher standard as they navigate the children of God through troubled waters and the storms of life. James 3:1-2. Preaching and teaching are not for everyone. Luke 12:48.

In the school of life, some are pupils, others are teachers. God calls and gifts a few people to be spiritual teachers. If a preacher stumbles, she often causes her students to stumble. Matthew 18:6-7. Those who do not stumble are considered as mature in their faith. Jude 24.

A teacher or a preacher affects eternity. Her personal influence never stops. Remember that James reminded his readers that not many should become teachers, warning that words can cause others to stumble.

The listener should leave church on Sunday not so impressed with what happened during the hour spent in church as what is going to happen because of that hour the hearer spent there. (Daniel D. Walker, *Enemy in the Pew*, p. 94)

Worship is part of the total preaching event. The setting will either contribute or distract. Prayer, music, litany, scripture reading, or a benediction or anthem will engage individual listeners. Nobody knows in advance through whom or through what God may choose to speak.

My lifetime mentor and friend, Dr. John Killinger wrote "The Pastor's Ten Commandments."

> I. Thou shalt love the Lord thy God with all thy heart and mind and soul, and thou shalt love thy parishioner as thyself.
>
> II. Thou shalt keep the worship and preaching of thy church strong and inspiring.
>
> III. Thou shalt work always at the peripheries of thy congregation.
>
> IV. Thou shalt forever attempt to get others to do thy work.
>
> V. Thou shalt hold on to what works and let go of what doesn't.
>
> VI. Thou shalt turn every meeting, however casual or unintended, into a pastoral occasion.
>
> VII. Thou shalt cherish the gifts of others and thy shalt imagine ways to use them.
>
> VIII. Thou shalt publicize, publicize, and publicize the people in the church and what they are doing for one another.
>
> IX. Thou shalt always be positive and upbuilding in thy speech and attitudes.

X. Thou shalt remember to say thanks for the gift of having a pastorate.

"When all is said and done, what richer place could there be for us to live our lives? Imagine having a family of hundreds of people, all caring about you, and the way you feel, inviting you into the inner sanctions of their lives, sharing their sorrows and joys with you, listening to your speeches, holding you up to God each day in prayer, and trying in their various ways to help you do your job. There is no other calling in the world quite like it. Where else could we feel as satisfied about the worth of what we are doing?

"It is natural to have our times of discouragement and despondency. If we didn't, we would think it was time to hold the devil's funeral. But as a whole it is hard to picture a profession in which the rewards are so precious and heartfelt." (John Killinger, *The Tender Shepherd*, pp. 200- 207)

When there is the technology, my congregations have enjoyed movie clips to illustrate a point in my sermon. I have purchased scores of copies of *Lights, Camera, Faith* for my preaching colleagues. The movies represent Cycle A of the Lectionary.

One delightful movie was Sister Act with Whoopi Goldberg, who plays Deloris Van Cartier, a singer in bars. She observes her gangster boyfriend commit a murder. For the witness protection program, she is placed in a dull and quiet convent. The nuns call her Sister Clarence.

Street smart and energetic, she clashes with the Mother Superior. She makes friends with other nuns. Preaching and worship in the convent are dull and drab.

With her gift of music, she is asked to direct the hapless choir. Only a handful of faithful Christians attend mass. Sister Clarence is quite creative. She uses non-traditional rock style hymns.

Showing her faithfulness, she urges the sisters to go beyond the walls of the convent to get involved in filling the needs of people.

Soon the congregation grows and grows. The attenders became a packed house. Ordinary community people, the mentally ill, addicts, blatant sinners, the poor, and the unwanted filled the congregation with joy.

Sister Clarence is spotted on the television news helping the marginalized by the gangsters. The gangsters sneak in and kidnap her. When she is snatched away, the nuns now know who she is. They go with the police to rescue her in Reno.

Back in the neighborhood of the convent, her choir has now become well-known. Even the Pope come for a visit. The film is high-spirited and a pure joy. Sister Clarence wears contemporary clothing with sexy red high heal shoes.

The message of this film is sharing the love and faith in Christ with everyone, no exceptions. The choir use secular songs, including "I Will Follow Him" and "My Guy." (Peter Malone and Rose Pacatte, *Lights Camera, Faith: A Movie Lover's Guide to Scripture, Cycle A*, pp. 294- 297)

This book on movies will stay on my shelves for preaching insight, information, and inspiration. The book is a challenge for preaching to use words and songs that common non-religious people can comprehend. Faithful preaching and worship not easy or casual work. It demands every ounce of strength. It demands a unique kind of creativity and full awareness of the cultural environment.

Unless she is called with these gifts from God, she can do nothing. Unless Jesus the Christ is invited to guide the preaching, preaching becomes a dull sham. Paul the Apostle was so committed to preaching that he was willing to go to prison for it. He said that he was an ambassador in bonds. He preached with faithful boldness.

Experimental preaching and worship provide a thought-provoking message into the world that is starved for Good News. Preaching today includes engagements of faith through a variety of cultures through the grace, love, joy, peace, and faithfulness. Isaiah 52:7.

The apostle aul ells Timothy that elders must be "able to teach." I Timothy 3:2. Titus 1:9. The only particular must demonstrate is the ability to teach. Does Paul mean to captivate an audience, to look good on the stage, to have charisma or charm.

"Able to Teach" Isn't About Rhetorical Ability

It is about preaching. Elders must be able to expound sound doctrine. Preaching is not the only context where preaching happens. "Able to teach" is to focus on the content. It is not just a gift of gab.

Paul used soundness over style. Paul means a person is able to faithfully and to apply the Bible, so listeners grow in the knowledge in a way that produces love of God and neighbor. Godliness in leadership is the point. It is better to do average preaching and have an impeccable character than a gifted preacher without character.

God does not require eloquence, bur faith, boldness, and faithfulness. As we thank God for divine faithfulness, let us be reminded that God requires faithfulness from us. Faithfulness is the most important quality needed in serving our Lord. God challenged the church at Smyrna to be faithful unto death. Revelation 2:10. Paul was willing to deny himself. Faithfulness to the Lord demands faithing attitudes. Most preachers today are not interesting in "decreasing." They aim to increase fame and fortune. They dream of living in the lap of luxury. They covet silver and gold for themselves. Paul disagreed. Acts 2:33-34.

Paul was never about trying to please any church authority. Three years was actually the longest time that Paul stayed to serve in one city throughout his ministry. Faithfully, he was able to teach both Jews and Greeks by preaching the word of God. The Ephesian church acquired a sound foundation. We all have a role to play in the kingdom of God.

Today Is Not the Day to Stop Preaching

Preaching is the means to faith, the way to salvation, the voice of Christ Jesus. Churches need a faithful pulpit. Whether we preach to two, two hundred, or two thousand, what comes from the pulpit is what matters. We need the Word of God. Churches need to proclaim it.

Jesus began his ministry by preaching. He "came into Galilee preaching the gospel from God." Mark 16:15.

We listen to the quiet voice of God spoke to the apostle Paul in a time of deep discouragement in Acts 18:9-10. This not the time to stop preaching.

There is an urgency for every person in the community to attend a church where the Word is faithfully preached. That has to do not just the honor of God and the Word. Preaching has the vital purpose of the salvation of souls. "The Word does not return void." Be faithful and preach with conviction, power, and relevance.

Dear readers, I hope you understand this. Your soul, and the salvation of your soul, is tied to the means that God has appointed, the preaching of the gospel. "By the foolishness of preaching to save them that believe" remains to please God. Please read my book, *The Joy of Preaching*, published by Parson's Porch several years ago. I want to encourage you to discover the joys of preaching in your faithful journey. Go where the joy is.

My dear servant. I came preaching. James, I perceive that you do too much trying to reach the world. Are you being completely faithful when you bring your anxiety and fear of not being and doing enough into your listeners' encounters with Me? There is no need for preaching in heaven.

Everything will be shouted from the rooftops eventually. I can make use of every fault and failure of yours when it turned over the Me. I like that
you preach with Me in places where my Word is needed such as the jails, the nursing homes, college campus settings, outdoor parks, and wherever My people gather.

Jim, you were born to be a preacher. Rejoice in My Word. Now that you are retired, I continue to delight in your faithfulness to sharing My joy. I know that when you were a young preacher you had visions of being one who could change the world.

By now despite the money and time you spent on preparation for ministry, you know that no human can be the source of changing the world. My Word pierces the heart and soul. Preaching opens people to discover their thoughts and intents through the power of My Word.

I never intended for My Word in the Scriptures just to stay on paper. Because of their depth, they must be opened and explained. Preaching is the power of salvation. Read Hebrews 4 and preach on it. That is want we want in preaching. The preacher is not just a lecturer. Preaching is not an address for your mind or emotions. Preaching is for the whole person.

My Holy Spirit awakens your faith inside your heart through preaching. It has this kind of power because Jesus, My Son, speaks. II Corinthians 5:20. In the preaching event, you do not hear the voice of another human. You never come just to hear a preacher. You come to hear Jesus speaking to you.

It is Christ's voice that calls a sinner to hear My call to repentance Only Christ can do that. That is My consolation for you. Let me be in control of your preaching and writing. Only then can your faithful work be extraordinarily relevant to the needs of your generation.

Chapter Eight

CONVERSION AND FAITHFULNESS

Conversion prevents faith from becoming static. It is not only a single act, but a life process. Conversion means a change in our way of thinking and the transformation of our inner attitudes. During the process of conversion, we turn away from evil and sin. Conversion turns spiritual death to life. Conversion is necessary because it is part of the solution to the serious nature of the human problem. Human beings become different when they are being converted. II Corinthians 5:17, Romans 6:14.

As soon as we were converted and transformed, connected to Christ by faith, sin was no longer our master. Sin has no enslaving power over us. In this life, we are troubled by sin. Romans 7:18. That is our experience as well. Martin Luther said we are "simultaneously saint and sinner." Our righteousness depends on our faith. Philippians 3:9. Christians live in this tension.

Struggling is normal. The Holy Spirit pushes us to trust Christ more. He is our only hope for peace. In the process of conversion, the Spirit is resurrecting us now with a taste of our future resurrection.

Our status is locked in the finished work of Jesus the Christ. Therefore, God sees us as righteous. Nothing can separate us from the love granted to us by grace. Christ comes and communes with us that we belong to him forever. We have no need to doubt our salvation. Our standing before God is secure. We are safe. Romans 5:1, 8:1.

Jesus said the kingdom of God is here. Mark 1:15. When we hear the word "repent" or "conversion, we think it applies to others. Conversion and faithfulness are lifelong processes. We all need to change. Nobody is perfect. Conversion is to become more like Christ.

To change our self-centered ways, we must not say, "What's in it for me?" Faithfulness means to change our need to have and buy things and take responsibility for other people and the world we live in.

Our attitudes of promoting conflict and war become promoting peace. Conversion is the soul and center of Christian faith. God loves and accepts us as we are. We have a deep hunger for God.

When we attempt to fill our spiritual center with things, substances, accomplishments, events, other people, our egos, we end up empty. Conversion is allowing God to control our lives.

Focus on the journey, not the destination. Joy is discovered not in finishing an activity but in doing it. Faithful conversion is to open ourselves to God as we make the necessary changes.

Conversion begins with the gracious gift of new life. "Saving faith" lights the spiritual fires by grace with repentance continues for our time on earth and eternity.

Jumpstart Faith

Leaping in faith without knowing where we might land on the other side is fearful. The leap is essential. Faith is the belief in something larger, grander, and more powerful than any person. We are guided by love. Faith builds bridges. The passionate love of God continues to pursue us. Leaping is choosing to abide in grace and love, or to go through life on our own.

The leap of faith shows a healthy vulnerability. We give up control. We cannot leap too early. We can leap too late. Bear Woznick, *Deep Adventure: The Way of Heroic Value*, pp. 1-192.

Conversion depends on the work of God in our lives. God initiates dealing with the human problem. When the Bible speaks of sin and humans as sinners, it is not a minor problem. Personal resole education, or self-help underestimate the problem. God demands that we are holy as God is holy.

If we fail to grasp something of God's holiness, perfect righteousness, we will not discover the importance of conversion. It comes in grace through faith. Conversion involves turning from sin and turning to Christ.

Faith Is Central to the Process of Conversion

Many times, when Jesus approached his disciples, it was due to their lack of faith. Questioning the apostles' faith was to lead them to conversion. Faithfulness leads us to question our own faith. Faith develops through the permanent process of our conversion.

Conversion begins with the gracious gift of new life. "Saving faith" lights the fires by grace with our repentance that continues throughout our lives. Given glimpses of concrete experiences of conversion, I have realized that conversion is a life experience that we know as it has been narrated. The experience has clearly changed lives.

This phenomenon has never ceased to be viewed as a spiritual integration and an invitation to begin living in faith. Conversion brings new dignity for the children of God.

Explaining conversion is not easy. It is more complex than the mechanical way we have been taught about "saving faith." Some communities believe God does it all. Theologians call this "predestination." Many Calvinistic groups teach that people are pre-chosen to special salvation from God's grace.

God continues to reveal thoughts of full submission of faith, mind, soul, and will. That is the leap of faith. To take this act of faith, the grace of God and the help of the Holy Spirit precedes and assists in opening our spiritual eyes of our souls.

Conversion begins when we stay present for love. I do not discount revivals, altar calls, joyous epiphanies, where the Spirit of God descends in a fiery flash. The Spirit comes in a fainted whisper that we completely miss unless we become intimate with God. Stop. Listen.

Many mature and faithful Christians think, speak, and write of conversion taking place in a single critical event. In the early church the language of conversion refers less to a single event, and more to the outcome of a process. Psalm 51:13.

The word for conversion in Hebrew means "to return" or "to go back." It means "to change the mind." Conversion becomes a lifelong process. Converts continue to serve and to speak the Supreme One's will with diligence.

There Is Never Ultimate Failure

The rising of Christ from the dead means there is no ultimate failure. No life is doomed. No evil is final. God extracts good from evil. When we stray from God, we can return. After every fall, remember God is waiting. God loves us through the gift of forgiveness.

When I lost the first manuscript of this book, my financial records, notes for four planned books for 2023, I had an epic meltdown in front of all the members of a book club that was meeting in my home. I gave each of them copies of my books for free. I had been twisted and devastated over my losses.

My retired old body was physically tired, emotionally drained, and spiritually depleted. The stress of being faithful to my calling as a preacher and a writer had turned into an idol.

All it took was a spark to ignite a fire like my meltdown because I lost sight of eternal faithfulness just because I had lost one book manuscript. Lukewarm in my faith, the fire I had for God was almost extinguished. Romans 12:2. I had done just what that verse was telling me not to do. After my meltdown, I realized I needed to make spiritual changes. I cried out to God in prayer in the process of my continuing conversion.

I had to ignite my love for Christ. To live with faithfulness means to see Jesus' loving and bestowing Presence. Because of faith Christ gradually becomes a light that shines in our transforming lives. Every moment, he is there. Yahweh links grace to every moment even if it during a difficult time. Acts 17:28.

Everything that happens in our lives is linked with grace. Faith places us in unity with the thinking of God. Faith overcomes pretenses. Faith helps us races of our creator. Without Christ we cannot know how we are loved. When we are aware that we are weak and sinful, we have the opportunity to be surrounded by Jesus' arms because he is the Good Shepherd, who looks for lost sheep and those who are helpless and weakened.

Faithing is gratitude for this never-ending love. We have little faith in God's continuing forgiveness. God constantly expresses forgiveness with joy. Conversion is difficult because there is too little contrition in our souls. Without it, faith is shallow. Revelation 3:15-16.

If we do not primarily seek the kingdom of God, everything else will be taken away. Matthew 6:33. It is a call from God for our conversion. God is jealous. Our creator loves us until the end. We must open ourselves fully for the spiritual gifts so that God can bestow everything on us.

Sooner or later, we will leave everything and detach from everything. It will be difficult to leave everything when we are in the last stages of death. God wants to save us from that pain. We are astonished about this reality that God's desire for our freedom is for our good.

Our faith journey does not have road maps. God can be quite confusing.

Our ways and thoughts are not God's ways and thoughts. Our work and our possessions do not define us. We must continually remind ourselves of our individual importance to God. People today are not fired but downsized. Applied to human beings, this concept is terrible.

Unique Specialness of Ordinary People

Every human being is special in the eyes of God. This fact is proven in our personalities, in our voices, in our faces, and our expression of thoughts. Even our fingerprints are extraordinary, a personal signature, duplicated by no other human being.

The genes in our cells that program us to become absolutely different from every other living creature. We are each one of a kind. This helps us move solidly ahead in our journeys of faith. We fail to see the riches coming from God to convert us into citizens of heaven.

Faithfulness comes with setbacks. Our smooth ride becomes bumpy when our expectations are dashed into pieces like my losing my plans for a book. We maintain faith in a seemingly faithless world. Church attendance rates are at an all-time low. Many denominations are forced to close churches as a result. People increasingly feel a lack of faith within the church communities. They feel it in their own lives.

Remaining faithfulness feels impossible when faith is absent from daily life. We must regularly examine our faith. Reflect on faith as introspection is essential. Prayer and journaling help. Current feelings echo other times of disconnection along life's journey.

Feeling alone and isolated, we identify with the faith stories in the biblical accounts. These stories of inspiring figures show the struggles we have experience to reconcile our faith beliefs with our doubt and outright hostility.

Jesus is the ultimate inspiration. He was rejected, despised, and ultimately killed. He knew loneliness like no other figure in history.

Conversion is a process. Having meltdowns is normal. Sometimes we exaggerate our losses because they mess up our personal expectations. My own expectation was that my book would bless my readers and bring more joy to the world. My plan was that when step one was done, step two would follow.

"The best laid plans of mice and men" are blitzed by things beyond our control. Faithfulness includes tolerance, adaptability, and flexibility.

My own faith has suffered detours for decades, followed by endless beginnings. Because we get uncomfortable, we passionately ask God for help. We question what life means. We long for heaven. Crises occur. We experience misunderstandings in marriage. Families fail to get along with each other. These things the beginning or deepening of bonds and love. Conversion is the work of Christ in us.

The word "conversion" appears only one time in the New Testament. Acts 15:3. Several words are used for converts. Change is the heart of conversion. To be converted is to have changed our thinking and believing about Jesus Christ.

Conversion means turning away from things that used to give us pleasure, love, and loyalty, and turning toward God to serve and trust our redeemer. The Word of God calls this repentance. Trusting God means depending on divine grace and promises for forgiveness and reconciliation through the gospel of Jesus. This is faith.

We are born again by the Holy Spirit, and we are given a new nature that loves God and desires to please the creator. A convert is someone whose change of allegiance and newness of heart means a change in our citizenship from the kingdom of this world to the kingdom of God. We are born into the family of God. We are changed inside by God. Faithfulness follows our lives inside. We declare and demonstrate that change outside through a life committed to following Jesus.

Theologically speaking, the doctrine of regeneration or conversion is where the Holy Spirit begins in our lives. Titus 3:5. The process of change, sanctification, continues throughout our life journey. Paul calls this being "in the Spirit." Romans 8:9. It is deep unio with Christ made possible by grace. The Holy Spirit dwells in the life of faithful believers. It is the ground for Christian hope. The seal of the Holy Spirit brings us assurance of final redemption. II Corinthians 1:22, Ephesians 1:13, 4:30. God the spirit shapes and conforms us to the image of God in Christ. Faithing is to be known by the fruit of the Spirit, not the works of our flesh. Galatians 5:19-23.

A convert is a disciple. Disciples follow because they have experienced conversion. Who is responsible for conversion? God is responsible for conversion and the individual is responsible to convert. Both play a role.

Conversion is first the work of God and then it is our work in faithfulness.

God has to work first, because we are dead in our sins. We are slaves of sin, enemies of God, under God's wrath, excluded from God's family and without hope. Because God works first to makes us new, otherwise conversion is impossible.

We must repent and in faith believe. God will not repent for us. God does not believe for us. Our repentance is a change of mind, belief, loyalty, and love. It is a complete orientation to keep the divine promises in Christ. God's prior work of regeneration enables our secondary work of repentance and faith. God gives the gift of faith by grace. Ephesians 2:8. God brings full life as new creatures in Christ whose nature is to turn toward God.

If conversion is the work of God to make us new, we cannot lose our salvation. We can no more change back into our old creature. We could never convert ourselves as we are dead with our sin. John 10:27-30.

Human Beings Radically Changed

Jesus promises that his sheep will hear his voice and follow him. Saving faith keeps believing. Persevering faith results from Jesus' faithfulness. Human nature can be radically and perfectly changed. By God's gifts of love and grace is always from the side of God.

Our hope is that our faith is in the Living God who constantly gifts us through others. God remains the constantly surprising Other.

Between faith professed and faith enacted lies discernment. God's call continues in changing circumstances. We cannot predict or control. Real life reveals that we never know which choice is right for us.

Every open-handed sharing of our possessions is from our faithfulness. This enacts faith's essence. Paul expressed this aspect of faith in II Corinthians 8:9. We are all spiritual creatures living in the condition of both being and having. How we dispose of our possessions symbolizes our spiritual commitments. Our possessions are far more than material things. I want my many sermons, books, recorded sermons, and all that symbolizes my work as Minister of Joy to the World to be given somewhere.

We let go of our ownership of anything on earth. Our response in faith is never just a one time. Faithfulness is faith responding to God during our lifetime. Being converted, we share our possessions and our faith with our families and community. We do not define ourselves by our individual possessions. How we share is determined by the discernment of the community that we encounter. The book of Micah writes about what pleases God. Micah 6:6-8.

Conversion Is Accomplished By God

When a person is awhile of sinfulness and alienation from God. Conversion is accomplished by God. The sinner feels guilt. That means the Holy Spirit has been at work in her life.

We must be faithful. The Holy Spirit is sovereign. Human faith and the grace of God. Matthew 25. The implication of the parable is that it does not matter how much we have given. What is important is how we respond. God has chosen to use human instruments to accomplish divine purposes. Andrew Bonar said, "No soul will be in heaven without a human thumbmark upon it." James Stewart, *Evangelism Without Apology*, p. 72)

Jesus assures us that he is holding on to us. Nothing will make us loose. Nobody can see inside a person to evaluate their heart, to see if they are a new person in Christ.

Sometimes people who gave every appearance of being converted will walk away from the faith, deny Jesus their Lord, and return to a life of sin.

We cannot convert anyone by ourselves. God must act or nothing happens. The Holy Spirit is not under our control. Our goal is not conversion, but it is the courageous, bold, and faithful sharing of the message of salvation.

This implies that if our goal is to be full of faithfulness instead of aiming toward our own success, causes us to be less tempted to resort to deceptive and manipulative practices.

The mark of a Christian is somebody who has repented and believed in the past, and who continues to repent and believe. That is their nature. When a person says that they have been converted stops living like one converted brings their witness into jeopardy. Matthew 18, I Corinthians 5. If someone has joined a congregation as a member who has gone through all the rituals and has been baptized upon profession of faith, but is not changing, God is not working in their life.

Conversion sets us free to be faithful evangelists. We are made part of the global mission. God is reconciling the world through the gospel. Assurance of salvation is grounded in the sincerity of our prayer. Look to Christ in repentance and faith. The more we infuse prayer into our routine, the more connected we are. Prayer can feel intimidating. Eloquence isn't required. We need not strive to say a perfect prayer. We can incorporate short, simple prayers into moments of each day. Our persistence will pay off.

It might take a few weeks or months before praying feels natural. Write reminders in your journal to keep on track.

Blessed is the faithful person who has undergone difficult experiences with God, who did not betray Christ, but who remained faithful and steadfast. Through our faith, we shall begin to absorb the thoughts and desires of our Redeemer and love like our Father in heaven does.

Conversion brings praise and a depth of love for God. Inexpressible joy delights our spirit. Conversion gives us grace that surrounds us, envelops us in the depth of glory. We sing, "My hope is built on nothing less than Jesus' blood and righteousness." Inexpressible joy comes when we are having a hard time, joy appears far away. When joy comes into our lives, even more joy surprises us. Joy is expansive. It feels like being in love. Conversion brings a sense of excitement at the beginning of each day.

Gratitude and appreciation continues deep in our souls. Joy knows no bounds. Joy from God is a fruit of the Spirit with variations in intensity. Some say the opposite of fear is love. Conversion brings us the reality that joy is a more positive opposite. Joy is a motivator. Joy is a sense of energized excitement. Joy brings constant certainty. Joy embraces love and peace.

When we are living in joy, people want to be near us. We are changed into wonders of feeling fulfilled and connected. It is a strong physical emotion. We feel free of control. Joy is extremely powerful, resilient, and flexible. It transforms everything. We are created with a natural state of joy that will be fully realized when we join God in heaven.

Joy makes every situation we experience in life easier. We have a pivotal point. A new foundation will stem from joy better than anything we could imagine.

Resting in our Lord is difficult with world-wide pandemics, violence, and unrest. Anxiety levels are much higher than normal. Whether your crisis is a global problem or simply the stress of managing your college experience, you can get through the current storm with your faith fully intact.

Our ultimate hope relies not on our circumstances, but in our God who is above it all. We have no words left when facing serious issues. The Holy Spirit makes intercession on our behalf. The spirit is standing in the wings.

Conversion is a mysterious power of gentleness. Life in Christ is perpetual. Salvation is continuous, uninterrupted, everlasting, and eternal. There is an intimacy in our salvation. It is a personal experience. It is joy as sharing it overflows with delight. The conversion of Paul on the road to Damascus is one model. Conversion is a public affair and a spiritual awakening. It is an inner experience.

The awakened convert suddenly feels transported out of a normal way of existing. They feel that they are now free, joyful, liberated. He ecstasy of that moment wears off with time. The event is a life-changing and transformative experience that gives life meaning, purpose, direction, and joy. The experience will never be erased from our memories. Followers of Jesus become less conflicted, less fearful, less confused, less shamed, less impatient. Conversion is a taste of heaven coming down and glory filling our souls.

Each step of faith brings a fire-glow to our movement and fire-fall to our souls. The journey of faith embraces the glory of what is to be revealed because the grace already granted. Meditate, not a whimsical clearing of our minds, but a spiritual discipline when we close out the world and focus on faithfulness.

We can find a quiet place with a notebook, pen, and favorite Bible. Acknowledge the presence of God. Choose to relax.

Faith affects every relationship. In the Old Testament we find "the just shall live by faith." Habakkuk 2:4. Saint Paul continued "to read the parchments," to stir his faithfulness.

The apostle Paul writes in II Timothy 3:1-5 of human character in the end times. Faithfulness hinges on what we value combined with commitment. We tend to be faithful to what we think is important. Holding faith to the course that God has laid out for us is not easy. There are a vast number of alluring attractions clamoring for our time and attention. This world is attractive to vulnerable human beings. Faithless means treacherous, disloyal, unreliable, unbelieving, unscrupulous, dishonest, undependable, and doubtful.

Faithlessness promotes self-centeredness. Advertising hammers away for us to gratify ourselves. Indulge yourselves, you are beautiful, sexy people, you're worth it. Swimming against the tide is never a possibility. If you are beautiful in body, thank God. If you are brilliant, thank God with your thoughts. Psalm 34:2-3.

It is beyond mystery and imagination to see what lies in the unseen future for believers because mercy has been bestowed. Believers find peace in trusting because of the love already given.

Believers glimpse salvation with delight. Weeping is not gone this side of eternity. Joy comes in the morning. John 17:17.

Faithful believers ask for continuing grace in the process, grace in our preparation, the growing, the going and the coming, the grace in the receiving, the purpose, and the joy.

Our conversion is a promising prelude to harvesting faith and heaven. And there is unconditional love, a grace fulfilled, and a joy that will never end.

My found soul, conversion is an ever-continuous process. It is a miracle that you surrendered yourself to Me. You know that you belong to Me. You gave up depression and I gave you joy. You gave up your hurtful past for a promised future You gave up your sense of worthlessness. You gave up hopelessness and helplessness for constant assurance.

You gave up friends who led you into danger, destruction, and disappointment and found Me and My faithful followers. You gave up your loneliness because I am always with you. You gave up your worries and anxiety for My peace which passes understanding.

You gave up your guilt and accepted My forgiveness. And My faithful friend, you can count on Me.

When you feel your heart raging to the point of anxious numbness, it is time to search again for My Holy Word. All things do work together for your good. You will not always understand why I keep on giving My blessings. I realize that you cannot find joy by yourself. I know that deep down in your soul, you desire My peace.

Myself in the Holy Spirit has traveled billions of miles in My children's shoes.

Here is My plan for you. Keep on giving your time and energy to Me and My working through you. Let go of the allurements this world entices you with vigor and effort. I will give you My incomprehensive joy.

Your conversion continues in My grace out of My love and your faithfulness. Enjoy Me and love Me now and forever in My heavenly home that I have prepared with a place for you.

Continue to meditate on your faithfulness to Me, and My faithfulness toward you. I am the One who saves the world. Let Me satisfy you from continuing to be restless.

Chapter Nine

WORKS AND FAITHFULNESS

The greatest tool God has given to us is to impact the world is our work. We wake up in the morning with hopes our actions will have purpose and faithfulness to glorify God. A woman or man of words and not deeds is like a garden full of weeds.

The work that humans do will find its destination before God who instituted it. Work has an eschatological perspective. Faith and work will be rewarded. Faithfulness means we need to use our earthly journey to do our best work well. God's gifts of work give us benefits that will last forever.

God created work for different purposes to be done in differing ways by different characters. God gave redemptive work, skilled and professional work, subsistence work, charity work, occupational work, social work, scientific work, and spiritual work.

Work becomes a bridge of relationship. We see the goodness of God. We know peace and joy. The apostle Paul showed the joys of his subsistence work. Acts 20:34-35. Christians must live from their work. II Thessalonians 3:10-13.

Failure to work denies us fellowship with God. Because we are redeemed, we must help redeem others. We are God's peace representatives in the workplace. The vision of God for redemptive work is to provide faithful people an understanding of the extent of their participation in faithful work. We redeem our work attitudes for the service of God. There is no way we can redeem others if we are not involved in meaningful work. Matthew 25:40.

Integrating faith with work demonstrates that Christians have a differing origin and destination. Integration of faith and work re-energizes the spirit of work. If work has lost value, human living has lost value. God considered creation work as service and worship.

Faithfulness and the Image of God

Faithfulness reflects the image of God in word and deed. The joy of living on earth is heaven ordered and divine directed. Jesus Christ is the head of the Christian family. He makes Christian faith a heavenly culture. So those living in a heavenly culture do heavenly work. This work was created with many options that we can choose from. God came in Jesus to teach us how to work. To work is to be fully human. Because God is pleased with work, our duty is to make work a thing of joy by bridging the gaps.

The fall of humankind degraded the work value and lowered its quality. Genesis 1:28, 2:15. The integration of faith and work focuses on both intrinsic and extrinsic values. Sin changed work from a joy to a toil. Work has become a burden not a blessing. Ever since, work has become the focus for achievement of personal goal, not service to God.

Redeemed people are in a position to redeem their work from the power of sin. Unfortunately work has been marred with disappointments, corruption, and displeasure. Regarding work as joy has been turned to pain and suffering.

Christians should understand that they are called for a purpose. They must understand their roles as instruments of transformation as Jesus was. People need to ask questions to satisfy the basis for a biblical and theological regarding faithfulness and work. These questions include: Why did God intend human beings to work? Why should people work and work well? How is work supposed to be rewarded?

People should work because the Creator was a worker. When God created humans, they were commissioned to work. Genesis 1:28. Whatever God created was "very good." We must work and work well. We must be aware of poor workmanship. God will not appreciate and reward bad work. God is never pleased with shoddy work. Half-hearted efforts and sloppy work does not honor God.

It has been made clear that work was to bring joy between God and human beings, and between human beings themselves. Most of the corruption taking place in private and public results from hiding and not being willing to take responsibility.

People want to control what does not belong to them. When they cannot do things the right way, they apply the easy way to make a living. This ends up sapping their souls. The essence of work is abused. Suffering follows. Genesis 3:17-19.

Our job description is to do our best to invest all of your life and work for the glory of God. Faith is knowing the dignity and work of all sorts of work. God loves and cares for the world through us. Pray that God will give you grace to be able to do everything for the glory of God.

Accept the imperfections of our work. Faith gives us an inner understanding without which work could be our destruction. Success could go to our heads. We should not become inflated during the times of prosperity. Bitterness and despondency result during times of adversity. Colossians 3:22-24.

Work is grounded and guided by the moral principles of God. We may be tempted to step on or over a colleague to get what we humans want. We are tempted to cut corners, elevate numbers, have impure motives, and shady practices.

These were orchestrated by us. We must share four values: To act with integrity, to be fair, to have fun, and to be socially responsible. Paul Stevens, *Taking Your Soul to Work, p. 57.*

As a result illicit business, crime, financial misappropriation, and these vices that appear to be "easy money," have become acceptable. Real and meaningful work becomes distorted.

Pray that we will find our needs are met as you meet the needs of others. Pray that we find our joys and happiness of those we serve, not just people-pleasing.

Faith comes alive by the simple, caring touch of another person. Faith is not alive just because we speak words. God acts in deeds. God surrounds us in every person ever born. We discover God through others. Be assured that God is seeking you. Pray for the kingdom of God to come. Pray for the will of God to be done on the earth as well as in heaven. Pray for the hope that we need to persevere in our works even when we doubt that we are making a dent in the problems that we with God's help, are trying to solve.

My comments are focused on helping my readers to understand salvation. Faith and works are not rivals. The Bible is absolutely clear that our works do not merit or earn the grace of God.

Good works performed by believers are not the basis of salvation. Salvation comes from faith in Christ alone. Good works are the evidence that one has received salvation. This glorious truth has flooded my soul. I write not as a dogmatist, wearing ecclesiastical robes of infallibility. I am an ordinary grateful child of God. The Holy Spirit seeks to give us all insight and light on a subject which has been viewed without understanding.

The relationship between faith and works is central to the division between churches, especially Catholic churches and many mainliners. Jesus emphasizes this truth through many of his parables and sayings. The apostle Paul argues explicitly against the inclusion of works as the basis for salvation. James argues against justification by works "and not by faith alone." His writing harmonizes with the rest of the New Testament. James still expects us to sin. He is combating faith without work, not faith alone as the foundation. Receiving Christ by faith through grace means giving up the right of self. The living, pulsating reality of God's indwelling springs up like an artesian well of heavenly glory. Our faithfulness is effortless with our working, because it just flows. This perfect love casts out fear.

Faith in Christ gives us completeness. We turn from imploring petitioning to our agonizing works. We find continuous assurance that as we receive the gift of God's salvation, we experience heavenly joy. We are privileged to enjoy the flow of rivers of living water that come from the throne of God. When our days become dark and heavy, we find our sufficiency not in human works, but in indiscernible faith.

Faith in the Lord Jesus Christ works by love.

Faith that justifies necessarily flowers into good works. Martin Luther, a Roman Catholic monk, believed in the interpretation of Paul in Romans. Differing understandings of the role of faith and works led the church into the Protestant Reformation.

I can't wait until you read this book. To be successful we only need to be God's definition of faithful. Writing a book is lonely work. I pray I have carefully used all the words needed to convey the message. I am sensitive to the Holy Spirit to serve with faithfulness. Ephesians 3:14-20.

I type on my computer with one finger as I have all my life. It is a letter- by-letter task. Deleting, changing, seeking a fresher way to express myself, I pray these words will fill another person with my works. Any deep wisdom is my gift from God. My work is to be faithful in the ways the divine writer desires to use me.

My supporting readers may never preach a sermon nor write a book. Those who read my work are called to do more than they can imagine. Stir up the gifts within you. There are amazing things that only you can do. First, your calling will be outside your comfort zone.

Christian faith and Christian deeds are the same. Faith and faithfulness are also the same. We can't have one without the other. Certain things go together. We know one by the other like salt and pepper, thunder and lightning, hugs and kisses, socks and shoes and peanut butter and jelly. James 2:14-18.

Faith without actions is useless. Faith by itself cannot save us. The problem with interpreting this Scripture is that so much of the Bible appears to say the opposite.

There are not enough good deeds we can do to gain entrance into heaven. Romans 3:28, Galatians 2:16, 21. Paul and James are discussing two different things. The Jews thought that they were the chosen ones of God. Paul is communicating with Jews. This problem confronts us today. That's the apostle Paul.

James is facing the opposite problem. That problem is lackadaisical faith. Lax faith. Lazy faith. Paul is talking to the Jews about laws and regulations. James is writing about acts of love. Paul is writing about what happens to us on the inside. James is writing about the outside. James is showing us the evidence for our experience of salvation.

Their readers are chasing the wind. They cannot see the wind. It is invisible but it does exist. Wind blows the branches of trees. Wind brings waves on a body of water. Wind can harness energy for power. Wind in abundance creates a hurricane.

James says faith alone is dead. James certainly knew the saving grace of faith. James 2:5. He says some people are rich in faith. James is not advocating deeds instead of faith. He says that there is no separation of faith and deeds.

James declares that the only way to have genuine faith is to demonstrate it with our deeds. Works are not added to faith, but faith includes works. Otherwise, it is useless and dead. James 2:19-26.

James' issue is faith being alive and real. Works do not produce faith. Works do not replace faith. Works validate faith. Works demonstrate faith. Works are necessary to show that faith is real. Romans 5:6-10.

We stand in grace through faith. This world is not our home. We have eternal life. Works are not a substitute for faith in the theology of James. Works validate faith. Faith is the essential ingredient for James.

Works do not eliminate faith. Works don't supersede faith. The only thing he is writing about works is because he wants to know if our faith is real and genuine.

Why should faithful Christians live in a certain way? It is to serve others because that is what Jesus did. We must live to be useful to God as Jesus was. To do works is to become like Christ. It is not to earn the God's favor.

Our works play a role in turning other souls to the gospel. Works help other people become believers. I Peter 1:10-12. People need to see a light in darkness. We are a model of good works. We are doing good works so that God will love us. That is so wrong.

James uses a horrible warning to humans who claim to have faith and yet have no deeds. They are indistinguishable from demons. Demons believe in God.

In Mark 5, there is the account of a man with an evil spirit inside of him named Legion. When this ill man saw Jesus, he shouted, "What do you want with me, Jesus, Son of the Most High God. Swear to God that you will not torture me." Demos know who Christ is. They do not possess a saving faith. Demons know who Christ is but continue to perform evil deeds. Their beliefs are correct, their behavior is not.

James uses the stories of both Abraham and Rahab to make his point. It does not matter who we are, from Abraham to Rahab, from respected patriarch to a redeemed prostitute, our faith must be perfected by our deeds. James writes that both Abraham and Rahab are declared righteous because of their deeds.

James is attempting to clarify exactly what faith is. When we interpret James, we observe that faith is not something we say or think, believe, or feel. It is not faith over against deeds. God wants us to demonstrate our faith because faithful demonstration means we trust God. And when we rust God, God strengthens our faith so we can do even more good works.

Justification by faith alone is interpreted to mean that works have no place in salvation. We blur the lines between justification and salvation. We do not appreciate the interconnection of faith and work. Let's consider how justification by faith alone is squared with works.

Justification is the eternal declaration of right-standing before God. Justification reconciles us to God. Some tend to think salvation happened "in the past." The New Testament speaks of salvation as a future reality. Some think being saved now is done, and there is no future judgment. Romans 5:6-10. Works are the fruit and evidence of obedience. Inward reality and outer expression in John the Baptist's preaching in the wilderness. Matthew 3:7-10.

John talks about the fruit, which focuses on repentance. Sometimes an obedient heart is called a repentant heart. Paul speaks of love as the fulfillment of the love of God. Mark 12:28-34, Galatians 5:14.

Scripture Affirms the Importance of Works

The importance of works is affirmed in the New Testament. We can interpret this to mean that eternal life result from works. There is a connection between our being forgiven and our forgiving others. Matthew 6:14-15, 7:21-23, 16:27. Here Jesus does not make a distinction, but he says that everyone will be repaid by their faithful actions. Read Matthew 25:31-46. Both groups of people refer to Jesus as Lord. In both cases the basis of their acceptance or rejection is their works. II Corinthians 5:9-10. Why do so many people believe in salvation by work? Many people expect God to evaluate us the same way we evaluate one another. As long as our good outweighs the bad, we will go on to heaven. This comes from the idea of "being good enough. The Bible is clear that doing good deeds is the result of salvation, not the basis of it. Ephesians 2:8-9.

God the Father is equated with the earthly fathers. Good was rewarded, bad was punished. We misunderstand God's role as Father as a Supreme Being to be pleased without understanding the importance of knowing God personally through faith in Jesus.

We desire a sense of control of our afterlife. Performing certain works is said to enable us to reach heaven. No one can perform well enough to achieve a perfect status before God. Romans 3:23. That is not God's expectation. We can't perform enough and that is why God came to earth in Jesus. Titus 3:5-8. Salvation and eternal life are not obtained by human effort. Revelation 1:5, John 3:6-7.

Grace is unmerited favor given to us through our faith. Romans 11:6. Personal righteous deeds are called "filthy rages." Romans 3:23. Salvation is a divine exchange of our tattered rags of self-effort for the purification of Christ.

Believers are God's workmanship, created in Christ Jesus. When we ae made new creatures in Christ, the desires we once had to live for ourselves and for the ways of the world change. Instead of pleasing self, we now live to please Christ and to glorify him. We are not saved by our good works, but we are saved for good works.

Do not approach God with your good deeds list. God notes our motives in serving. Our works are as filthy rags if we are not concerned with sinfulness and the meek. These deeds are without honor in the darkness that is mirrored in our souls. Just rest in love, joy, and grace. There is not one thing that we must do.

Only God can bring change into our lives. Confessing Christ or professing faith in Jesus without our changing, without being dead in our sins to new life. Apart from Christ, we can do nothing. John 15:5.

Good works glorify God and serve others. There is joy in this truth. Colossians 3:17. In my prayer and support groups, I find it helpful to have companions who are seeking to be faithful. Our experiences of being led by the Spirit to works that are unique to each one. In our support for each other we discern the Spirit's leadership. We find what causes us to resist. Opening ourselves to inner and outer support enables us to live faithful lives.

A 35-year-old Nebraska farmer said, "How can we find God? God is all around us. The essence of our existence. Looking at God's creation, we see the work of the Almighty Hand. I find God in the soil I till, the crops I grow, the water I use—all working to provide food. I see God in other people through their acts of kindness. I believe you can find God in the way the universe functions, in the intricate way it operates. If you have faith, all you have to do is open your eyes and God is easy to find." (Antoinette Bosco, *Hanging in There When God Seems So Far Away*, p. 92)

Works link with faithfulness as we show faith by what we do, not what we say. Faith sees Christ in everyone. Matthew 25. God wants our walk and talk to match. We improve our faith walk by attaining a living faith that practices what it preaches. (Lenya Heitzig and Penny Rose, *Live Faithfully: A Study in the Book of James*, p. 17)

Only time will tell whether one is an authentic fruit-bearing Christian. It is impossible to determine faith by outward appearances. God wants spiritual fruit, not religious nuts. Galatians 6:7.

George Blondin was a tightrope walker. He lived back in the 1860's. For a stunt to gain publicity, he decided to walk across Niagara Falls on a tightrope. Starting out slowly, he walked carefully inch by inch until he reached the middle. Everybody who was watching knew that one little step would plunge him down the falls to certain death.

When he finally reached the other side, the crowd roared wildly. George Blondin said, "I am going to do it again." This time he would push a wheelbarrow filled with dirt. He did this a total of four times. One woman said, "Wow. How incredible. I really believe that you could do that all day." The tightrope walker dumped all the dirt out of the wheelbarrow and said, "Get in."

An empty faith is no faith at all. Empty faith is a working faith. Salvation comes by faith plus works. Paul dealt with this truth many times. Some have said that salvation comes by intellectual faith alone. James and Paul wrote that faith alone is worthless. It is dead. It is like demon faith.

Christians who focus on deeds are burdened with an expectation to do more. They faith to depend on the grace of God. Those who focus on faith without works are pious, useless, and any of their obedience produces sanctification.

Salvation comes with genuine faith that finds evidence by our deeds. Faith and works are not separate. They are one thing intertwined. We have been asked, "If you were arrested for being a Christian, would there be enough evidence to convict you?"

The Christian walk involves receiving gifts, repenting of all filthiness, reproducing righteousness through doing the will of God, and examining life in light of God's vision for humankind.

God has sown something amazing in the soil of our souls. We must make our hearts more fertile by doing what God desires. The book of James teaches that inward conversion shows outwardly in righteous speech. James 1:27.

The Works of Paramedics Saves Lives

In our little town of Elmwood, Nebraska, we hear the sirens screaming and the firetrucks and police cars. Paramedics rush a citizen to the emergency room in a Lincoln or Omaha hospital. "We got a code blue, a flatline." Quickly physicians access the patient. The doctors then pull-out defibrillation paddles, sending bursts of electricity into the body to shock the heart into activity. The patient is hooked up to an EKG to measure heart rate. The doctor pulls out her stethoscope and listens to the breathing to make sure the lungs are working. When the crisis is averted, the patient survives.

We need heart and lungs to live. Without both functioning properly, we die. The Spirit needs two things to function together: faith and work. Without them, faith becomes flat-line, faith that is dead. James 2:15-17. James used a hypothetical situation to reflect the lifelessness of faith without work.

Jesus himself expects us to be obedient and to express our faith with deeds. Christ said, "Why call me, Lord, Lord, and do not what I say." Matthew 7:21.

Working from home has brought some unique challenges. In recent years, I observed many impacts on my work. My theology of work is doing "Immanuel labor." God is present wherever we work. God has not changed. God continues to work inside me, with me, and through me. While working alone in my office, I feel the presence of my Lord.

None of us know how our "new normal" will last. I find it harder to make decisions when my supporters are scattered. I have been forced to learn how to do work outside my comfort zones. I have not been face to face with my publisher in the years I have worked with him. My present environment brings me a higher level of discipline. How I submit to my publisher's worldwide ministry in a tangible way from a distance becomes critical. Sharing faith is the best way to develop faithfulness. Faith is an intimate, personal decision. It is also lived with a strong community dimension. The single reality of faith that we ae in communion with each other. Ephesians 4:4-6.

Faith is received and transmitted. Joy of faith is in celebration. Proclaim and sings faithfully together. Faith cannot be kept inside your heart. Encouragement from testimonies of faith from faithful sisters and brothers is so essential. Romans 1:11-12.

If we conserve our faith, limiting it to just a little corner of our lives as a private matter. If we never witness t, and declare it, there is a strong risk that faith will wither.

Witnessing our faith must be humble and respective toward others. Never give up an opportunity to share your faith. Only the Holy Spirit can open hearts. Witnessing our faith will always result in our growing stronger with grace and faith.

The apostles kept the faith in the way they had received it. They gave it away. Their faith was precious. They had full confidence in grace, love, joy, and faith.

As the weeks of teleworking turns into months and years, I work harder to find ways to connect.

Ephesians 2:8-10 expresses the summary of the question about faith and deeds. Grace brings saving faith for a life of doing good works. God is preparing us to do just that. That is surely what God wants from us.

The Gospel of John emphasizes the importance of faith. He used the Greek verb for "to believe" 98 times to underscore faith's vital importance. The Jews asked about what they must do to perform God's works. John 6:28. Jesus answered them by saying to "believe in the one he has sent." John 6:29.

Joy of Eternal Life

John emphasizes repeatedly that those who believe enjoy eternal life. John 1:12, 3:16, 5:24. A person is not saved by working for God, but she or he is saved by believing in God.

A light that does not shine, a spring that does not flow, a seed that does not glow is not more strange that eternal life in Christ does not witness.

Learn to share your faith. Start by making conversation so that ordinary evangelism counts.

We need facts and clarity about our faith. Jot down the events of importance in the life of being faithful. Start with your confession of faith and baptism.

Note the holy moments that surprised you with joy and brought you closer to God. Contrast these moments with moments of disappointment when we find ourselves far from the Lord.

Keeping a journal keeps us aware. We are ready for any opportunity to share our conversion story. We can share the compassion and mercy of God with others. Our own struggles and failures brings us a maturity of spirit. We will then have a burning desire to use our talents, training, and graces to share joy that lives inside of us.

Most of us can remember a Sunday when nothing was supposed to happen. On that day the Holy Spirit moved people to accept Christ by faith.

Astounding and Unexpected Joy

We will see the results in others. And we will experience the joy of the Lord in astounding and unexpected ways. Each one of us has a gift from God. That gift is guided by the Holy Spirit. My work has the foundation of I Peter 3:15-16. This book is an expression of my desire to share my own faith and joy, and more about one another, more about ourselves and the intimate love of God.

Conversion means that we share the joy of the Lord that is alive in our souls. Every work we do as ministers of joy to the world is a celebration of joy. I find joy in conversations and in speaking to church and secular groups.

My sermons and my writing and my counseling have the purpose of inspiring you to share the stories of your faith to interact with others seeking the same love and grace. Remain focused on Christ. Some Christians have fallen into the trap of becoming argumentative with empty talkers which leads people nowhere. Give the simple gospel, love people and never forget that we cannot argue people into heaven, the kingdom of God.

Pass it on. It only takes a spark to keep a fire burning. Start your unique journey with someone today.

James, you know one of My other followers and a writer of my Word in the book of James said that faith without works is dead. You have poured out wells of delight in living Your salvation. Your glad response is willing and exuberant to be My hands as well as My heart in this troubled world.

It is I who points out the needs that can be met by your work and faithful deeds. Grace, love, and joy in salvation needs practical avenues, urgent longing to be with Me among the hurting and suffering.

Knowing Me frees you. Worldly pitfalls trap you. I offer you an escape into My kingdom. Join yourself with other believers by doing My work.

Often, I see you attempting more than you can handle. Remember that resting in Me is an essential part of doing good deeds. I forgive you of everything including your excesses of overextending and under-evaluating or failing to look at Me for guidance and balanced living. Look at My Kingdom concerns first, and I will enable you to learn to make peace with priorities and experience patience in your work of well-doing.

Stop being so concerned about your place in your world. I have set you in the right place for you. I give you nights of restful sleep. I awaken you with a morning of renewed refreshment.

I will lead you to be faithful and honorable as you do your deeds. You will not return to your nightly sleep time feeling shame or guilt. I shall give you sustenance as you labor in well doing. I shall guard you from yielding to temptation. I will be there to help you avoid the paths that emphasize the peripheral, miss My imperative. I will cause your heart to be sensitive to your work in this time and place where I have placed you.

I shall show you what matters most. I have graced your life with many benefits. Allow your work to bless others. Deepen your faith in Me. I want your faithfulness to include moments for you to relate to hers, to work and accomplish good deeds, to relax, and keep praying with Me.

I must slow you down to a pace in working in your will and not your frenzy that keeps you from thinking and praying. I shall fill your rushed moments with My calmness and peace.

Chapter Ten

HEAVEN AND FAITHFULNESS

Earth is the place where we touch heaven. Life, not death, determines whether we continue self-love or enjoy heaven. Life is where we become who we are, and where we are placed on earth is our only place where we touch heaven. When humans touch heaven, heaven changes life into joy and grace and peace. If we have the Spirit of God through faith in Christ, there is an incredible future that we have never heard, nor seen, or ever imagined.

Imagine that a child was born and grew up in a house with no windows. Grass, buildings, trees, birds, animals, and sunshine would never be seen. This little child has a disease that does not allow him to go outside. One day somebody takes him to a room with a window. He sees life and the blue sky, but he cannot go outside.

We have been given a window for us to know that there is something outside of us beyond where we are. Making sense from a temporal, time bound perspective, life seems meaningless. Ecclesiastes 3:11.

Confines by space and time, we have only one way to see beyond where we are. Faith and faithing give us a window on eternity. Ephesians 1:15- 23.

Paul describes what God has done through grace, love, and faith for our eternal salvation. Paul lets us see through a clear window the riches of the love and grace of God. Ephesians 1:13-14. Paul continues to expand in verses 15-23, offering a prayer for us to know an eternal. Perspective on God's work in heaven offering a window on heaven.

Paul gives us hope in what God has been doing, giving us a spirit of wisdom and revelation in our knowledge of our Creator. We become confident that God will complete what was done through Christ. The apostle wanted believers to know the riches of God's glorious inheritance in the saints. We share in Christ's resurrection glory. This is far more than we can imagine.

Paul writes for us to know the immeasurable greatness of the power of God. Faith, according to Paul, gives us an eternal perspective. This eternal perspective, this window on eternity, makes all the difference how we view reality, how we view our relationship with God and with others.

We face limitations and liabilities, trails and temptations that come from living in a fallen world within time and space. It's easy to get tunnel vision. Things that appear as major are minor, like a blip on a radar screen. God will incorporate it and use it in God's grand eternal purpose in Christ.

A Nebraska farmer found a wounded young bald eagle. He took the bird home. He nursed it to health. Later, he place it in with his chickens. The eaglet grew to adulthood but was scratching as chickens do. His wife commented on how sad it was to see it acting as a chicken. He placed the bird on a high post.

The eagle could use its keen eyes to glaze the sky as it caught a glimpse of heaven. Finally, the eagle soared into the air where it belonged.

Joy Known Here on Earth

It is not a temporal joy experienced one time. Eternal joy is known here on earth. We will totally experience in heaven is joy that will come from God. Scripture gives us a small glimpse. Isaiah 51:11, Psalm 84, Revelation 21:3-4.

Heavenly living is living in the heavenly will of God here on earth as it is in heaven. Heaven and faithfulness are connected. They lead us into heavenly living every moment of each day. Surrounded by the ungodly ways of this world, we fall short of the glory of God. We are finite creatures. God is infinite.

Jesus said our focus must be on him. Matthew 6:19-20. As we live each day, we anticipate our heaving home. Joy is a byproduct of the indwelling Holy Spirit. Joy molds and shapes our soul. Joy emanates from Jesus Christ alone. Joy faithfully fills us when earthly pleasures fade away. John 15:9-11.

The prescription for having complete joy is to be faithful in our faithfulness in his love and grace. Paul and Barnabas never stopped preaching despite the opposition of the Jews. Paul and Barnabas were expelled from the region around Antioch. Acts 13:49-52. Both we and other Christians engaged in the things that brought glory to God. Christians abide in God's love. When I professed faith in Jesus as an eight-year-old during Vacation Bible School at Woodlawn Baptist Church in Bristol, Tennessee, I became a lover of Jesus.

A Vision and the Fire of God

I know I received the fire of the Holy Spirit as I prayed. I became committed to Jesus. I was his willing vessel. I had the desire to pray for others. During Lottie Moon mission weeks, I prayed for the world to know the joy of the Lord. Our Father in heaven wants every person to know how much they are loved.

The fire of God and this vision quest was beyond reason and logic. Jeremiah 33:3. By faith, especially at night, I had the sensation that God wanted more personal encounters with me. In times of quietness with few distractions, God has spoken to me, and I have learned to listen. Places and people are shaken in faithfulness. Bodies feel physical responses in the presence of the Lord. Daniel 10:7, Psalm 99:1, 114:7, Habakkuk 3:16, Matthew 28:4, Acts 4:31.

I have seen enough, and all it has to offer, but all this pales in the light of God's heavenly vision. Psalm 18:1-3. I never feel lonely. I don't need other people's company. There is such joy in encountering God.

There is no easy way to our continuing faithfulness. To please our Lord, we must submit everything, including the things we don't want to give up. We do it because we love in the grace of God.

Heaven is not only a philosophical concept. It is not a sentimental dream. It is an actual place. Heaven is more real than where we presently live. It is a place from which Christ came into his world. It is the place where Christ Jesus returned.

Heavenly living here on earth is the ideal we are all seeking. In the kingdom of heaven, there is no suffering, death, or strife. Matthew 20:1-6. This is just how God created Eden. Think of the scripture as an example of the Lord hiring us to follow Christ and heavenly living among other people.

Everyone receives the same Holy Spirit and the same salvation. Nobody complains about their salvation, or about someone else being saved. Faithful ones are incited with joy.

Have you ever wondered what brings God's joy? The joy of the Lord comes when we work in marriages that reflect Christ, this beings joy to God. When we raise our children in the fear and guidance of God this brings joy.

One thing that brings God joy is that those who are lost are found. Luke 15:2, 5. With eight billion people who live on earth this very hour, and even innumerable numbers whom God created, we feel we are not that special.

Jesus wants us to experience the joy that the Father experiences. Joy is incited when one human being finds salvation. This is how God feels as you are being saved.

God's joy is our reward. Matthew 25:21, 23. We are offered our Master's joy. God knows joy because of our fate and faithfulness. God offers that eternal joy as a heavenly reward. Isaiah 62:5. God rejoices over us the way that a groom rejoices over his bride.

Heavenly Living and Worldly Living

The difference between heavenly living and worldly living is described by Paul. Philippians 1:20-30. Paul is looking beyond heavenly living on earth to actually living in heaven.

Worldly leaders who are bound to worldly living want to kill Paul. They see the apostle as a threat. Paul is torn between allowing himself to die assuring that he will be with the Lord or remaining in his ministry journey on earth.

Heavenly living is the focus of Paul. He is experiencing evil forces at work in this world. Living in the heavenly will of God is to do all that we can to free life from its present corrupted condition.

Heaven is where God lives. Focus on Psalm 33:13-14, Isaiah 63:15, Matthew 5:16, 45; 6:1, 7:11, 21; Revelation 3:12, 21:10. The house of God is related by Jesus in Matthew 10:32-33. This was the sense that Jesus referred to heaven throughout his ministry.

It is more than a mystical notion. It is not an imaginary dreamland. It is the place where God the Creator lives. Hebrews calls it a distant country, where those listed in the hall of fame lives. Hebrews 11:13-16.

When we speak of heaven, we are referring to a place. When we talk about eternity, we are speaking about an era or an eternal state. Heaven exists now even though we are not experiencing it. Eternity is a future dimension of time without an ending. Heaven exists now and will continue to exist throughout eternity.

Dark Days and Heaven

The image of the new heavenly Jerusalem numbs people in the darkness and storms. Life becomes confusing and painful in the deadly and dangerous earth. Jesus is making a new world. Every tear will be wiped way. Death will be no more. Dark days will become a distant memory.

As a pastor, I was asked by children, "Pastor, what is heaven like?" They wonder how their parent's ashes that were thrown into the river will be put back together. Grandpa was cremated and his ashes were spread throughout his favorite golf course.

During an experience of joy, we say that we are in heaven. Heaven is the most misunderstood n our language. We now see through a glass darkly, as the apostle Paul wrote.

There will be new heights to climb, new depths to go down to experience the joy of the profound. This gives us a spring in our step. Love will be forever. Love's places distinct. Love is superior to hope and faith in heaven.

The superiority of love is clear. Love excels in an extraordinary way. It is a way of excellence. Other wonderful things will come in the future. Love is matchless.

God has given us foretastes of heaven. The Garden of Eden is a foretaste of paradise. In Eden, there was a perfect relationship that was harmonious with all creation. The church can be a foretaste of the joy of fellowship and worship in heaven. Glimmers of golden light, whispers of angelic refrains, bring whispers and whiffs of heaven. Hebrews 12:22-23.

Sometimes we are afraid of our senses. Too much joy and too much enjoyment is not pleasing to the demands of God. Faith clarifies that to little enjoyment stops our progress and displeases our Father. No person has ever been condemned for having too much love. None will ever be condemned for having too much joy. We speak on all our emotions in bodily terms. We say to keep the chin up, kept a stiff upper lip, be hard- nosed, that is a pain in the neck, grit your teeth, or have guts.

Some hold theories of joy that means "getting out of our bodies." Actually, full joy is felt when we are most aware of our bodies. With an experience of joy, we are more aware of all that is around us.

Shared communion gives us another glimpse of heaven. Matthew 26. We will share a wedding feast in heaven. Revelation 19:9.

The Holy Spirit is another foretaste. The Spirit of God is our inheritance. Ephesians 1:13-14. The Spirit assures us of blessings to come. We are the children of God. Hebrews 6:4-5.

Eternal Life Begins Now

Eternal life begins now. We have crossed from death to life. I John 5:11-12. We already live in the suburbs of heaven. We sing, "Blessed assurance, Jesus is mine. O what a foretaste of glory that will be. (Fanny Crosby, "Blessed Assurance, Jesus Is Mine," *The United Methodist Hymnal*, hymn number 369)

Faith is not just about whether God or heaven exist. As we behold the image in the Word of God in intimacy in prayer, knowing the Supreme Being as we reflect the image in ourselves.

That is the reason why a testimony of faith and faithfulness gives a feeling that feels familiar. Perhaps it is a subconscious recall from before our birth. We felt joy in our preexistence as the earth was being created for lingers within us. Joy comes through our faithfulness. Faith is not complete knowledge of the ways of the Holy Spirit.

The joy of faith is the joy of making it on your own finding answers we have not been given. Everything is worth more when done by faith with grace. That is the ultimate joy of salvation.

That mirrored reflection gives us incredible understanding. God is within our reach. We reflect heaven on earth. Recognizing the elusive but faithful friend we are in divine mysterious Presence beyond human comprehension. Life is a wonderful mystery. Dark times are difficult, but life is a journey of joy.

Miracles happen when heaven touches earth. Miracles are not miracles to God. Our vision for touching heaven is seen in the transfiguration.

Matthew 17:1-2. Jesus' face shone like the sun. His clothing appeared as white as that light. Peter, James, John, and Jesus also saw that light.

When they came down from the mountain, they soon went down into the valley. Mountain-top experiences are unforgettable. Like heaven itself, these high mountain-top times bring us infinite joy. Joy connects to a life journey that is much bigger than us.

God has gifted us to know the heavenly language of the lambs. We know the voice of the Shepherd, and what songs of pain and praise we might not know. We know a Shepherd who does.

When Jesus sends out 70 disciples to proclaim his message, he tells them upon their return to "rejoice and be glad, for your reward is great in heaven." He exhorts us to "seek first the kingdom of heaven."

Jesus teaches us that we were created to have joy because joy is linked to heaven. Christ assures us that no matter what happens, no matter how many our losses are, no matter how broken we are, no matter how much we are mired in grief, we are filled with joy because joy connects with the eternal.

William Wordsworth wrote, "With the deep power of joy, we see the God of things." (William Wordsworth, *Selected Poetry*, p. 54)

Faithful Christians wonder about heaven. As the next place is filled with beauty, joy, love, and endless peace. We will meet or reconnect with some interesting people. They will be in an eternal friendship with us. Living with our creator in wonderful worship and in an environment of meaningful work will be beyond anything we can imagine.

In my faith as a child and in my current faith I think heaven is a physical and spiritual place occupied with the souls and renewed bodies who will live with Jesus forever. Joy is child-like and filled with spontaneous delight. We are all born that way. Gradually we lose the surprising delights of joy. If you want a demonstration of joy, just watch the child.

Heaven is God's Garden of Grace, fragrant with the joy of heavenly love. Most of us believe in some kind of afterlife. We owe our children and our congregations nothing but the truth. When I preach a series of sermons on the subject of heaven, some looked stunned as I tackled themes such as, "Will There Be Sex in Heaven?"

It is difficult to imagine heaven as unending, unimaginable, impossible, and joyful. In my preaching and writing, I write in an environment where we live and die. There is a difference between believing that heaven exists and planning how to journey there. The most helpful sermon about heaven that I have read was by C.S. Lewis. He named it, "The Weight of Glory." Lewis deals with the question of motives. The Oxford scholar says we love ourselves naturally. God made it possible for us to love our Creator by joining with our nature.

Each of us is unique. Some things about God are appreciated and communicated. Light is special. There are aspects of God that you and you alone will deeply know. When our children or grandchildren ask us about our faith in heaven, we need to be truthful so that they can digest it for themselves.

We who hunger after God live in the joy of our Lord. Perhaps we can connect God in the name Yahweh to make us more comfortable with those who bristle with calling God him or her.

Travel has been my passion since I spend three summers in distant states as a summer home missionary during the 1960s. My first ministry trip was when I served as a graduate assistant at Baylor University, was a mission to conduct a revival in Mexico. During my platinum jubilee of 70 years of preaching, I have shared the joy of Yahweh on all seven continents.

Before I plan, write dozens of letters and emails, I want to know all I can about my next destination. II Peter 3:13. Our anticipation, excitement, and joy are ignited as we seek to know what we are able to know. Heaven is a place that is worthy of our thoughts, hopes, and dreams.

Heaven is a place revealed in unseen glimpses in the Holy Scripture. Many people, including life-long scholars, doubt that heaven is a physical place. They might think we have eternal souls. Yahweh did not create us to live like ghostly spirits. If we have faith in Jesus, we shall enter the present heaven, the new earth, when we die.

Jesus promises that he will bring us back with him in what is called the Second Coming. A new and Eden-like paradise with water, animals, land, trees and flowers much like we know today. Today's earth yields pleasant and unpleasant surprises and every kind of emotion like fear, anger, guilt, anxiety, and joy. Joy is all we need to experience in heaven. Joy means that we have touched God. Knowing joy is knowing heaven. Joy connects us with the eternal.

If we have not found God on earth, we will not find our creator in heaven. Heaven was not created as an escape from problems. Heaven, Jesus says, is already inside us.

The apostle Paul gave us insight that the kingdom in contrast to the present time of understanding as seeing darkly as through a mirror has been smeared with dirt.

Heaven is all around us. It is an intensification of the faithful image of a place that is the best we could know in our lifetime. We will never discover heaven if we do not do the work of Christ in our world where need is camouflaged. That work is feeding the hunger, clothing the naked, and visiting those who are in prison.

Jesus is present when we respond to these needs. Our affluent society can easily ignore the poor. We insulate ourselves from them and heaven as well. Affluence indicates that we have much to share.

Faith involves seeing the needs and faithfully doing the work. The prize for this work is heaven. Most faithful Christian writers want to be more eloquent in paining vivid word-pictures of faithfulness in God's incredible world.

Writing Ministry Produces Odes of Joy

Our writing is an ode to God who put life and joy in us forever. This surely is the love of God. We are created in that love and rested on the groundwork of this reality.

Faithfulness opens our eyes to know God's Prescence. We move out of the darkness that prevents us from seeing heaven is within our reach.

Faith tells us God is everywhere. Heaven comes without our invitations, simply out of the unconditional love and grace. It cannot stay without our invitation. The time to invite the joy of heaven in is now. Today is the accepted time.

Joy means we have touched God. Knowing joy is knowing heaven. Joy is exultant satisfaction. Joy is the inexpressible state of being that connects us to God. Creation was made for joy, and it is linked to the creation of heaven. Joy is eternal.

Faithing brings us what we can understand about heaven. When our journey on earth ends, we will be in familiar territory. Faithful Christians do not enjoy the best in this life. Life gives them little reward.

Feelings bring us experiences that connect us to life beyond this world. We long for fellowship with God. This grows with the passing of years. There must be a heaven. Faith tells us with confidence in the Holy Scripture. If we doubt it, the whole system is distorted. Jesus clearly spoke of mansions, places for every faithful believer.

There is a heavenly city whose builder is God. There is a heaven. Faith declares it so. Following the blueprint of Jesus, we build heaven beginning on earth. Matthew 25:31-40. We can see the face of God in every person we encounter. The circle of life has God at the center. There is no beginning and no end.

Our Heavenly Home is being Prepared.

Heaven is a prepared place, not just an accidental conglomeration. God as the architect has built it out of love. It is a thing of beauty, a joy forever. There will be no need for prisons, hospitals, nursing homes, or for most professionals including preachers. Heaven is a populated place. John says there will be so many that no person can number. The citizens will include every nation. The marriage feat will include 144,000 which means God's perfect number. Millions have accepted the invitation.

The apostle Paul declares "our citizenship is in heaven." Philippians 3:20. It is beyond earth. Heaven is in existence now. It has been the dwelling place of God since eternity past. God is not limited to heaven. God's omnipresence makes it possible to be anywhere at any time. I Kings 8:27.

Heaven is God's habitation. It is a unique home where the divine throne resides. Heaven is extra-physical. It surpasses all our concepts.

Our mothers and faithers, sisters and brothers, husbands and wives, sons and daughter will have journeyed to heaven. They will be there waiting for us. God has given an appetite for eternal love.

There will be no flaws, no mistakes, no discouragements, no disappointments, no sorrow, no pain, or no suffering. We will never grow old. Waters in the river of life will flow freely. By faith and grace, I know that I am going there. Faith gives me the assurance with my soul singing, quiet sounds in my mind beyond question.

With my own faithfulness, I believe in the Lord Jesus Christ. I have confessed Jesus beyond women and men. All my sins are forgiven. My name is written in the Lamb's Book of Life. I am sealed in eternal love. All along my journey since I accepted Jesus s my personal redeemer, God continues to have provision for me. In faith, I have been given the gift of the Holy Spirit to empower my faithfulness. I have proved again and again the words of my first sermon from Matthew 6:33. In the Kingdom of God, all things will be given to you on this earth and in heaven.

The Gates of Heaven Swing Open

Today the gates of heaven swing open. The Holy Spirit is whispering gently my welcome to the invitation. This is what Jesus is doing for me. I feel the Presence. I am beginning my journey into heaven. I will not call my faith finished. I shall spend the remaining days of my earthly life doing my own faithful work. I shall affirm my graceful and loving, gentle and joyful position with the Holy Spirit. There will be no tears in heaven, just smiles and great joy.

My desire for you, my dear readers and supporters, is that you will celebrate your first birthday of your converted soul face to face with Jesus and all your loved ones.

Faithfulness is an eternal love song. God sounds the notes. Faith provides the score. Faithfulness is never silent. (Michael Barrett, *The Silent Stream*, p. 12) The hymn, "Great Is Thy Faithfulness," was written during a deep and heavy darkness. Jeremiah wrote these comforting words in the middle of the Old Testament prophecy. Lamentations, disappointment, horrors and regrets fill most of the writing.

Faith happens as we journey with God's open door. God is bread when we are hungry. God is water when we are thirsty. God is our harbor during the storms of life. God is light in our darkness. Faith helps us understand the grace and love of the Supreme Being. It is more than mysterious and beyond our imagination. William Wordsworth wrote, "With the deep power of joy, we see into the God of things." God lives in this world. Open the door and see.

Rainbows are a sign of connection with our loved ones and our loving Creator. Genesis 9:13, 16. God is faithful. The divine light for our journey has just one requirement: Respond with the faith of a child. Faithfulness drenches us in peace and an incredible sense of joy. This joy is a sign of God in us. Joy is our connection to heaven. What difference does heaven make? Some of us already live in different worlds. We sit on the porch studying in the Bible about heaven. We go to bed visualizing heavenly Zion. We reflect on tings above. Most think and act in thoughts of things below.
Those who think about heaven do the greatest work on earth. Keeping heaven on our minds keeps hope in our souls and hearts and the Good News on our lips.

Heaven is the continuation of God's eternal purpose on earth. God has a purpose for heaven. Heaven is for restoration of the glory of all creation.

Psalm 16:11. We are called to be God's representatives.

Enjoy heaven now. Mother Teresa lived to be 100 years old. She said, "If I ever become a saint, I will surely be one of darkness. I will continually be absent from heaven to light the light of those in darkness on earth." (Brian Kolodiejchuk, editor, p. 414)

Those of us who have lived 80 or more years remember watching the Mary Tyler Moore Show on television. Heaven comes for those who have endured. Remember the program's lyrics.

"Who can turn the world on with her smile? Who can take a nothing day and suddenly make it all seem worthwhile?

"Well, it's you girl and you should know it. Each and every moment you show it.

"Love is all around. No need to waste it. You can never tell why you don't take it? You're going to make it after all."

At times as my faith was shaken, I was assured that nothing is too difficult for God. God is eternally acting inside of you. "You're going to make it after all."

My heavenly brother, faith overcomes the world. There are many worlds for My faithful ones. There is the inner world of your own soul. There is the world of your close family and friends. There is the world of the flesh, entertainment, business, and politics. Let Me be your God.

I have an unimaginable world prepared for you. You are a part of My arms stretched out to comfort those in need. You ae part of My voice making justice plain. I show you ways to walk in peace. Hold on to the heavenly atmosphere, and love with overcome any obstacles.

Heaven results from My breath pulsing in you. Filled with Me, you put on the apron and serve Me from your respect, genuine love, and your heavenly desires.

I have given you a mind for learning. Your life is full of variety and possibility. Your world is filled with beauty. I have provided you with opportunities that deepen and broaden you. Loved ones inspire you. Your soul, Jim, is filled with gentleness, sensitivity and searching. My blessings are innumerable as the sands in the ocean.

I know you have been stunned at times, because you see Me as through a muddy old mirror. My joy in you in heaven is beyond understanding. Your faith and My grace give you a whisper of what My servant Paul wrote. Your desire and love for Me stir in your soul. It shall never end.

As your heart longs for My perfect love, it will be filled. Your hands must reach for it. Your feet faithfully walk with Me in the pathway of righteousness.

Earth comes closer to heaven when people live in Me and I in them. I have unconditionally loved My creation. I want to bless you and everything I have made. You are not called to follow other Christians. You are called to follow only me. Take your eyes off all My other children.

Together as Faither and son, we will step out on the front line. Your faith will become an adventure, because you will be focused on your eternal purpose. Don't allow anybody else's actions to alter your own course of action. Live out what you know is My calling to you alone. Don't place your faith in My children. Nobody is perfect. Keep your eyes on me. I am perfect.

My son, I can see how much compassion you have for others. My heart aches for those who are hurting. My coming for all people is quite near. Souls are saved in My joy and strength.

I want the world to know that I am a fearsome God. I have always loved My children. That is why I died for them. Everyone needs to repent and become humble before me. There will always be distractions on earth until I come for My people. Really, I want you to repent daily. I do not want anyone to miss the trumpet sound.

Jim, you could never love me more than I love you.

Your earthly vision of heaven is dimmed. May your soul long for being with Me. I will bestow vision to your weary eyes. I will give purpose in your seeking. I'll watch as your hands do good deeds. My thoughts will become your thoughts. In My love, I shall keep and use you.

I have been saying to you that you must seek Me first. I am to be your focus. When I am pleased, there will be miracles. These will be My miracles, not yours. Never forget that your faithfulness is important to Me.

Whoever loves worldly things and their families more than me will hurt Me. Jim, it was Me who opened every door for you to use your talents in ministry. I have blessed you.

I have chosen you for a specific work. Just as your years of preaching, praying, teaching, counseling, and writing has been beyond your childhood imagination, exciting beyond words. I have chosen you to bear everlasting fruit.

The world can become of harmony, love, and peace. I know what it is like to be a human being. I suffered just like they do. Even a lot more than you imagine. I came down from heaven. I am in the Holy Spirit who yearns for you to be with me in heaven.

BIBLIOGRAPHY

Alcorn, Randy. "Looking Forward to a Heaven We Can Imagine," *The Gospel Coalition*, March 9, 2015.

Barrett, Michael. *The Silent Stream*. Plainfield, Connecticut: Serenity Press, 2009.

Barth, Karl. *The Word of God and the Word of Man*. New York: Harper and Row, 1967.

Berkhof, Enrickus. *The Doctrine of the Holy Spirit*. Richmond: John Knox Press, 1964.

Bosco, Antoinette. *Hanging in There When God Seems Far Away*. Mystic, Connecticut: Twenty-Third Publications, 2005.

Boyer, Ernest. *A Way in the World: Family Life as a Spiritual Discipline*. San Francisco: Harper & Row, 1988.

Brooks, Phillips. *Lectures on Preaching*. Grand Rapids, Michigan: Baker Book House, 1969.

Brown, Robert McAfee. *Is Faith Obsolete?* Philadelphia: Westminster Press, 1980.

Brueggeman, Walter. *Praying the Psalms*. Winona, Minnesota: Saint Mary's Press, 1999.

Buttrick, George. *Prayer*. New York: Abingdon Press, 1962.

Cairns, Earle E. *Christianity Through the Centuries*. Grand Rapids, Michigan: Zondervan Publishing House, 1994.

Carson, D.A. *Faith and Faithfulness*. Deerfield, Illinois: Ligonier, 2020.

Cox, Harvey. *The Feast of Fools: A Theological Essay in Festivity and Fantasy*. Cambridge, Massachusetts: Harvard University Press, 1970.

Craddock, Fred B. *Preaching*. Nashville: Abingdon Press, 1985.

De'Arcy, Paula. *Crossing the Threshold: Crossing the Inner Barrier to Deeper Love.* New York: Crossroad, 2006.

Dunn, J.D. "Faith and Faithfulness," *The New Interpreter's Dictionary of the Bible.* Nashville: Abingdon Press, 2007.

Farmer, H. H. *The Servant of the Word.* New York: Charles Scribner and Sons, 1942.

Forsyth, P. T. *Positive Preaching and the Modern Mind.* London: Independent Press, 1960.

Fosdick, Harry Emerson. *The Living of These Days: An Autobiography.* New York: Harper and Row, 1956.

Griffith, Leonard. *The Need to Preach.* London: Hodder and Stoughton, Limited, 1971.

Gutierrez, Gustavo. *We Drink from Our Own Wells: The Spiritual Journey of a People.* Maryknoll, New York: Orbus Books, 1988.

Fosdick, Harry Emerson. *The Meaning of Prayer.* New York: Association Press, 1915.

Fosdick, Harry Emerson, "What's the Matter with Preaching?" *Harper's Magazine,* 157 (July 1928) pp. 133-141.

Harrison, Ken. *A Daring Faith in a Cowardly World: Live a Life Without Waste, Regret, or Anything Unfinished.* San Francisco: Harper & Row, 2020.

Haselden, Kyle. *Morality and the Mass Media.* Nashville: Broadman Press, 1968.

Hebert, Gabriel. "Faith and Faithfulness," *Reformed Theology Review.* Melbourne, Victoria, Australia, volume 4, 1955.

Heitzig, Lenya and Penny Rose. *Live Faithfully: A Study in the Book of James.* Eastbourne, England: Kingsway Communications, 2015.

Hendry, John. *The Book of Forgiving: The Fourfold Path for Healing Ourselves and Our World.* London, England: William Collins Publishers, 2017.

Hinson, Glenn. *Seekers After Mature Faith*. Nashville: Broadman Press, 1977.

Holloway, Richard. *On Forgiveness: How Can We Forgive the Unforgivable?* Edinburgh, Scotland: Canongate Publishing Company, 2019.

Howden, Newton. *Life Here and Hereafter*. Sewanee, Tennessee: Proctor's Hall Press, 1998.

Hulme, William E. *Am I Losing My Faith?* Philadelphia: Fortress Press, 1971.

Hunsinger, George, "From the Great Cloud of Witnesses," *Weavings: A Journal of the Christian Spiritual Life*, volume II, number 2, pp. 26-29.

Jowett, John Henry. *The Preacher: His Life and Work*. New York: Doran, 1912.

Killinger, John. *Beginning Prayer*. Nashville: Upper Room Books, 2012.

Killinger, John. *Bread for the Wilderness, Wine for the Journey*. Waco, Texas: Word Books, 1976.

Killinger, John. *The Centrality of Preaching in the Total Task of the Ministry*. Waco, Texas: Word Books, 1969.

Killinger, John. *The Changing Shape of Our Salvation*. New York: Crossroad, 2007.

Killinger, John. *The Salvation Tree*. San Francisco: Harper & Row, 1973.

Killinger, John. *The Tender Shepherd: A Practical Guide for Today's Pastor*. Nashville: Abingdon Press, 1985.

Knox, John. *The Integrity of Preaching*. New York: Harper and Row, 1967.

Kolodiejchuk, Brian. *Mother Teresa Come Be My Light: The Private Writings of the Saint of Calcutta*. New York: Doubleday, 2017.

Kornfield, Jack. *A Path with Heart: A Guide through the Perils and Promises of Spiritual Life*. New York: Bantam Books, 1998.

Lewis, C. S. *Mere Christianity*. New York: Macmillan Publishing Company, 1964.

Lloydjones, D. Martyn. *Spiritual Depression: Its Causes and Cures*. Grand Rapids, Michigan: Eerdmans, 1965.

Malcomson, William L. *The Preaching Event*. Philadelphia: The Westminster Press, 1968.

Malone, Peter and Rose Pacatte. *Lights, Camera, Faith: A Movie Lover's Guide to Scripture, Cycle A*. Boston: Pauline Books and Media, 1999.

McFague, Sallie. *The Body of God: An Ecological Theology*. Minneapolis: Fortress Press, 1993.

McKaughan, D.J. "On the Value of Faith and Faithfulness," *International Philosophy of Religion*. Cambridge: University of Cambridge Press, volume 81, 2017.

McReynolds, James E. *Dancing with God: A Theology of Joy*. Cleveland, Tennessee: Parson's Porch Books, 2016.

McReynolds, James E. *Faithfulness in the Church: A Commentary on I and II Thessalonians*. Lincoln, Nebraska: University Press, 1973.

McReynolds, James E. *Joy Comes in the Mourning: Love Is Forever*. Cleveland, Tennessee: Parson's Porch Books, 2020.

McReynolds. James E. *Joy in the Seasons of Life*. Cleveland, Tennessee: Parson's Porch Books, 2020.

McReynolds, James E. *Passionate Joy: Building a Wealth of Joy in a World Starved for Love*. Shanghai: Universe Books, 2006.

McReynolds, James E. *The Gospel of Joy*. Cleveland, Tennessee: Parson's Porch Books, 2023.

McReynolds, James E. *The Joy of Prayer: The Way to Intimacy with God*. Cleveland, Tennessee: Parson's Porch Books, 2020.

McReynolds, James E. *The Joy of Preaching: Encountering Jesus through the Word of God*. Cleveland Tennessee: Parson's Porch Books, 2013.

McReynolds, James E. *The Spirituality of Joy: The Least Discussed Human Emotion*. Cleveland, Tennessee: Parson's Porch Books, 2011.

McReynolds, James E. *Visionquest of Joy: The Least Discussed Human Emotion.* Bryn Mawr, Pennsylvania: Dorrance and Company, Incorporated, 1988.

McReynolds, James E. *Walking with God in the Garden.* Cleveland, Tennessee: Parson's Porch Books, 2021.

Merton, Thomas. *New Seeds of Contemplation.* New York: New Directions Book Publishing, 2020.

Miller, Calvin. *Cultivating Spirt-Given Character.* Nashville: Thomas Nelson, Incorporated, 1989.

Niebuhr, H. Reichard. *Pathways to Faith.* New York: Harper and Row, 1963.

Ostendorf, Marel von. *The Theory of Faithfulness.* Amsterdam: Meerters Institute Publishing Company, 2018.

Palmer, Parker. *To Know as We Are Known: A Spirituality of Education.* San Francisco: Harper and Row, 1983.

Peale, Norman Vincent and Kenneth Blanchard. *The Power of Ethical Management.* New York: William Morrow, 1988.

Rice, Rebbekah and Daniel McKaughan, Daniel Howard, "Approaches to Faith," International Journal for Philosophy of Religion, 81, number 1, pp. 1-6, 2021.

Skipworth, Bonni. *Pirouettes, Pathways, and Prayers.* Locust Grove, Georgia: Laurus Books, 2012.

Starkey, Lycurgus M. *The Holy Spirit at Work in the Church.* New York: Abingdon Press, 1965.

Stevens, Paul. *Taking Your Soul to Work: Overcoming the Seven Deadly Sins of the Workplace.* Grand Rapids, Michigan: Eerdmans Publishing House, 2014.

Stewart, James. *Evangelism Without Apology.* Grand Rapids, Michigan: Kregel Publications, 1961.

Stewart, James. *Heralds of God.* Grand Rapids, Michigan: Baker Book House, 1973.

The United Methodist Hymnal. Nashville: The United Methodist Publishing

House, 1989.

Thielicke, Helmut. *The Trouble with the Church: A Call for Renewal.* New York: Harper and Row, 1965.

Tillich, Paul. "Communicating the Christian Message," *Theology of Culture.* New York: Oxford University Press, 1959.

Walker, Daniel D. *Enemy in the Pew.* New York: Harper and Row, 1967.

Ward, Ronald A. "Worship: The New Testament Basis," *Baker's Dictionary of Practical Theology.* Grand Rapids, Michigan: Baker Book House, 1967.

Westerdorf, John. *Building God's People in a Materialistic Society.* New York: Seabury Press, 1989.

White, John. *The Fight: A Practical Handbook for Christian Living.* Downers Grove, Illinois: InterVarsity Press, 1976.

Wink, Walter. *The Bible in Human Transformation.* Philadelphia: Fortress Press, 1973.

Wordsworth, William. *Selected Poetry.* Mark Van Doren, editor. New York: Modern Library, Random House, 1950.

Woznick, Bear. *Deep Adventure: The Way of Heroic Virtue.* Manchester, New Hampshire: Sophia Institute Press, 2021.

Zweig, Connie. *The Inner Work of Age: Shifting from Role to Soul.* New York: Simon & Schuster, 2022

ABOUT THE AUTHOR

James McReynolds was born and raised in East Tennessee. Faith and family are most important to him. This book reflects on how to cope when your life lies in pieces around you. How do you rebuild in the face of all that you have lost? Nothing is too difficult for God. This book seeks to assure us that we will make it after all.

Jim lives in the small town of Elmwood, Nebraska with his wife Laurel. His email is joyminister@windstream.net.

OTHER BOOKS BY JAMES MCREYNOLDS
PUBLISHED BY PARSON'S PORCH BOOKS, 2010-2023

The Spirituality of Joy: The Least Discussed Human Emotion

The Joy of Preaching: Encountering Jesus through the Word of God

Dancing with God: A Theology of Joy

The Silence of the Church: The Spiritual Struggle with Sexuality

The Spirit of Joy Church

Great Is Thy Faithfulness: When Your Faith Is Shaken

Joy Comes in the Morning: Love Is Forever

The Joy of Prayer: The Way of Intimacy with God Envisioning the Great Commission:

The Joy of the Kingdom

Walking in the Garden with God

Joy in the Seasons of Life

Living the Dream: Amazing Adventure in Marriage

Joy Beyond the Walls of This World: Healing the Souls of Men and Women

The Gospel of Joy: Global Impact of the Ministry of Joy to the World

Joy Filled Souls: It Is Well with My Soul

Grace Revealed to Bring Joy to the World

Peace That Passes Understanding

The Strength of Being Tender

Great Is Thy Faithfulness: When Your Faith Is Shaken

Inciting Joy: The Magic of Ordinary People

www.ingramcontent.com/pod-product-compliance
Lightning Source LLC
Chambersburg PA
CBHW071405120626
46546CB00002B/818